Tunnel Kids

El Boston and Vero (La Fanta)

Tunnel Kids

TEXT BY Lawrence J. Taylor

PHOTOS BY Maeve Hickey

The University of Arizona Press

Tucson, Arizona

First Printing
The University of Arizona Press
© 2001 The Arizona Board of Regents
All rights reserved
♾ This book is printed on acid-free, archival-quality paper.
Manufactured in the United States of America
06   05   04   03   02   01   6   5   4   3   2   1

Library of Congress Cataloging-in-Publication Data
Taylor, Lawrence J.
Tunnel kids / text by Lawrence J. Taylor ; photos by Maeve Hickey.
p.   cm.
"First Printing."
ISBN 0-8165-1925-0 (cloth : alk. paper) —
ISBN 0-8165-1926-9 (pbk. : alk. paper)
1. Street children—Mexico—Nogales (Nogales)
2. Teenagers—Mexico—Nogales (Nogales)—Social conditions.
I. Hickey, Maeve.   II. Title.
HV887 .M62 N647 2001
305.235'0972'17—dc21   00-009122

British Library Cataloguing-in-Publication Data
A catalogue record for this book is available from the British Library.

For Daria and Tommy

"What are you doing in the river, you foolish boy? . . . Has no one ever told you, you will drown if you play in deep water?"

"Sir!" cried the boy loudly, as he felt himself sinking. "Please help me first, and scold me later!"

"A Boy Bathing," *Aesop's Fables*

Of course the Neverland had been make-believe in those days, but it was real now, and there were no night-lights, and it was getting darker every moment.

Peter Pan and Wendy, J. M. Barrie

Contents

ILLUSTRATIONS

PREFACE

Las aguas / The Waters

The noon skies turned midnight black and cracked open, roaring with lightening. The summer monsoons had come at last to this southwestern desert. We just made it onto the bus, three of the younger kids and I, but the windows would not close, and the weather followed us in. First came the sheets of rain— soaking stoic adults and ecstatic children—then the hail, like silver bullets from some army of drunken outlaws, bouncing off the green vinyl seats and into our laps. David and Gordito rushed from window to window, pointing with delight. Outside, water was everywhere, cascading down the steep hillsides from rooftop to rooftop, roaring through the *avenidas,* turning parking lots into ponds. We made it back to Mi Nueva Casa by the border, where it had already stopped raining. The streets down there were far less flooded, but the water was still on its way down the hills, as I discovered twenty minutes later when I tried to walk the few hundred yards to the border gate. The roads were gone, replaced by raging rapids three feet deep, black with muck and heaving sticks and plastic jugs into my legs as I staggered from one pole or building side to the next. I waded through a final swirling eddy, where a young woman clasping an infant to her breast balanced uncertainly on a battered shopping cart. Past the turnstile into the United States, I climbed the higher streets of Nogales, Arizona, where I had left my car. Safely on my way north toward Tubac, I remembered the tunnel and tried to imagine what the rains had brought to it. I heard the story the next day from Chito, who, along with many others, had been too far inside the silent gloom to hear the thunder.

"We were deep inside, in the tunnel they call 'Los Vampiros'—the one that goes through Buenos Aires. All of sudden we heard noise, and some people came running; they had been crossing to the other side. There were about fifteen. And then we heard a wave behind them. They shouted, 'Here comes the water!'" Chito undulated his arms to imitate the flood waves.

"And the next thing I knew, firemen, police, and *la migra* [Border Patrol] starting coming, and they grabbed us and pulled us up. There were many in the water, and many people were on the other side. The migra took a few of my friends and put them in a room, so I ran for the border."

Flushed into the United States.

A few days later it was raining again, and this time I took my car through the low streets of Nogales, Sonora. Afraid of more floods, I tore out of the house and tip-toed across the swirling, stinking pond that had in twenty minutes filled Avenida Fenochio, climbed into my car, and plowed a wake through Calle Capillo, driving north a few hundred yards to the border. But it was just an average summer afternoon rain, enough to send a few inches of brown water flowing through the border streets. Safely across on the drier Arizona roads, I thought of Chito and the others, and pulled up to the U.S. end of the tunnel, where it opens up into the concrete embankments of the Nogales Wash, just past Church's Chicken on Grand Avenue.

Leaning over the guardrail, I looked down into the opening—the scene of Chito's rescue a few days earlier. Chocolate water about a foot and a half deep was rushing through the large rectangular opening, just big enough for a car to drive through. I saw a sneaker flash in the gloom, then the pale smiling face of Chito "of the flood." The others were there, too: El Boston, La Fanta, Jesús Pecas, El Negro, La Negra, Humberto, Gilberto, and two little boys of about eleven and eight whom I did not yet know. They came grinning into the day-light, flashing Barrio Libre gang signs, and pushing a soccer ball through the churning rapids. They formed a circle in the open tunnel and began to knee, head, and throw the ball around—laughing and falling in the water. They were like any group of exuberant teenagers enjoying a summer rain. "Lorenzo," they shouted up to me, "*¿No tiene el video?*"—"Don't you have the video?" I obliged, taking a film of their water sports that they would often ask to see in the coming months.

This book is about these kids—a few of the twenty or thirty ado-lescents who work and sometimes live in the miles-long drainage tunnels that connect both the twin cities of Nogales, Sonora, and Nogales, Arizona, and the two countries, Mexico and the United States. They have come here from many parts of Mexico because of the border and the tunnel, so this book is also about the world that brought them together and in which they find ways to make a place of their own. It is their story of themselves and of the border, and it is our story of them—of getting to know them—and of the border as it appeared to us through their lives.

"Ambos Nogales"—Both Nogales—is one of several pairs of "twin" cities along the two-thousand-mile border between the United States and Mexico. Twins, but not identical. In fact, at times they appear to be as different as two towns can be—the third and first worlds face to face or back to back across a fence. The widely spaced homes on the American side and the familiar fast food icons such as McDonald's and Burger King sharply contrast with the chaos of the crowded, color-ful, decaying, jumping world on the other side. But that difference can be deceptive. Up the hills on the American side are also barrios from which cars loaded with bales of marijuana are followed to the supermarket parking lots by the vigilant Border Patrol. And Nogales, Arizona, is mostly Mexican or Mexican American (the distinction can be a very subtle one here). It is unusual to hear English in the Mc-Donald's on the border or in the Church's Chicken a mile into the United States.

In most respects, Ambos Nogales is like so many of the Mexican border towns. On the U.S. side, merchants depend on Mexican day-trip customers. The purchasing power of these customers rises and, more often, falls with the value of the peso. The Mexican side appears impoverished to American eyes but is an enterprise zone for the poor as well as for the investors building the *maquiladoras*. In these assembly plants, the typically foreign owners make fortunes and a small number of Mexican and foreign middle managers make salaries good enough to allow them to live in suburban houses in the Arizona "resort" community of Rio Rico. The thousands of workers earn only four to six dollars a day, but that is substantially more than they can get in the south, if and when such jobs are available there. And, of course, there is the tempting proximity of the United States, with its lucrative trade in drugs and human beings, and the possibility of immigration, legal or not. So the population of Nogales, like that of many Mexican border towns, has climbed exponentially over the last decades. By most reasonable estimates, close to three hundred thousand people live there, and certainly the vast majority in the *colonias*—a chaos of shacks spreading like a persistent rash over the hillsides surrounding the narrow valley of the original town.

Above the ground, this pulsing poverty is separated from the United States by a fence of changing materials. A small section of the current version—a high wall of recycled Vietnam War corrugated metal landing strips—has been recently replaced with a more aesthetic stone-and-glass, architect-designed affair. However pleasant, this pseudo shopping mall wall guards only a few hundred yards of our southern edge, giving way to the far less grand fencing that divides the desert to the east and west.

But the greater irony is below. The two cities, the two nations, are organically linked by two parallel tunnels—a sort of concrete urinary tract—each fourteen feet wide, about seven feet high, and several miles long. One, less used, has a permanently flowing stream of shallow water in the center; the other is dry—except, of course, when it rains. They are there to drain the summer waters from Nogales, Sonora, but given the less than hygienic state of that city, they also carry dirt and waste of every description. The entrances are always filthy; after rains, however, they are choked with stinking heaps of black mud, broken shopping carts, and plastic oil bottles. This distinctive feature of the Nogales border is both home and workplace for the "tunnel kids."

But these kids have another "home" as well, Mi Nueva Casa, My New House. We first discovered this place in our travels through the region for the book *The Road to Mexico*. The tunnel kids had been in the news, and some local people recommended that we visit a newly created "halfway house" that had been built for them. You can walk there from the United States, crossing the border at the gate and turning right. Six blocks farther along the fence, past the groups of men hawking taxis and the taco stands redolent with searing *cebollitas* (scallions), you come to Avenida Fenochio. On the corner, only yards from the fence, is Mi Nueva Casa—two tiny adobe row homes, three rooms each. We first entered in the company of then Santa Cruz County Attorney Jan Smith Florez, who, along with County Manager Dennis Miller, had conceived of the house and program. Creatively funded by American money—Arizona state funds for the prevention of juvenile delinquency and private donations—the Casa was intended to draw the kids from their world of streets and tunnel into an ordered domesticity. The American organizers, like Victorian reformers, hoped that a parlor would civilize these savage children.

The Casa had, in fact, a series of purposeful rooms. On one side was a little schoolroom with donated textbooks, a storeroom for supplies, and a game room nearly filled by the foosball table—the scene of many noisy and hotly contested matches. The main living space was on the other side, including a living room with a television and an assortment of tired sofas and chairs, a dining room, and a kitchen. That central room was presided over by two harried Mexican *madres* of indeterminate age: Doñas Ramona and Loida. About a dozen teenagers were regulars there. They showed up most mornings for breakfast. Afterward, they would take some remedial school lessons when a teacher was available, eat lunch, and sometimes engage in an organized activity, but most often they would simply hang out, watch TV, and wash their clothes. The house had no sleeping facilities, so in the late afternoon they all would leave and head either for the tunnel, the street, or the shacks of family or friends.

They showed little sign of ever permanently leaving the tunnel, however. Why should they, with no attractive alternatives? Not only were they making money there, but the tunnel was what made them special—to themselves and to others. The television newsmagazine *20/20* had done a brief but dramatic segment on their lives, a kind of *Les Misérables* of the border. Nobody was paying attention to the homeless Mexican children all over the country or even to those of the border region. The tunnel kids, however, were a story. They evoked a horror and pity that went beyond their immediate circumstances, resonating, no doubt, with the fantasies and nightmares of those of us who live on the surface. They were the dark underside—the hidden truth of the border. Their very presence and movement beneath it belied the authority, the reality, of any fence or wall. The "tunnel rats," as they began to be called, moved through the tunnel with the refuse and sewage of another country. They were themselves a living contamination.

If Americans were interested in the tunnel kids, from whatever mixture of fear or pity, the kids were smart enough to figure that out. They saw that the thousands of poor and homeless children of the colonias were ignored, while they received attention, however fleeting and sporadic. They understood that it was the tunnel that excited outsiders' interest and imagination, and the kids seemed to agree. They, too, felt the tunnel made them special. It was a distinctive and separate world that they controlled. It was dangerous, but it was interesting. It was even fun. For all these reasons and because the offerings of Mi Nueva Casa were limited and discontinued when the kids reached the age of eighteen, they were not likely to abandon the tunnel. Rather, they had made the house a useful part of their daily routine: a fueling, resting, and washing station between tunnel and shack.

In any case, for Maeve and me, the house provided a way in, a place to get to know the kids slowly. We returned to the Casa the next summer, trying to help as much as we could. Maeve spent time with the girls especially, and I began to take them all to a municipal pool to swim. Eventually we decided to return with the aim of putting together a book about the kids. We ended up spending nearly every day of a third and fourth summer with them—at first in the Casa, but eventually all over Nogales and sometimes far beyond. Although kids came and went in that period, the group had a surprisingly stable core, with El Boston at the center, along with his little pal Jesús and La Flor, Jesús' girlfriend and the mother of six-month-old Davidcito by a former boyfriend. They and others—wild Negra, poetic Guanatos, moody Romel and his beautiful girlfriend La Fanta, pale and ironic Chito, quiet Negro, morose Juanito, and flamboyant La Halloween (to name only some of the central characters)—shared part of their lives with us. We wanted to see and understand something of their story, but also, through them, the human dimension of the border.

Maeve photographed, taking pictures not only of the kids, but with them. Over the months she taught them how to use four different types of cameras and perhaps how to see their world through them. She also took a series of formal portraits, the tiny concrete courtyard behind the house serving as her "studio." Chito, in particular, was taken with the enterprise and would station himself near her with a huge umbrella to block the intense, blanching sun. "Next victim!" he would shout into the dark interior of the house, and little Toñito would stand between the door and the tripod, saving it from trampling teenagers.

For myself, I wanted to find a way to use writing to the same end and eventually persuaded a few of the kids to write a kind of autobiographical journal. I also brought a video camera, hoping that they (like kids elsewhere) would be drawn to that medium and through it perhaps communicate both with me and with each other.

The result of all this activity lies before you. The text is an account of a necessarily arbitrary sequence of events and adventures in lives that existed before and continued after this brief time we spent together. The photographs are equally crystallized moments in Maeve's relationship with the kids. From the brief stillness of the moment, they gaze out at her and at you, choosing to reveal one or another aspect of self. It is a self that often contrasts with that performed in other circumstances—the portraits providing a calm, haunting counterpoint to the sometimes frenetic pace depicted in the text, another aspect of the kids' complex humanity. Together, story and photographs, we hope, open a window into the life of the tunnel kids—the created world of Barrio Libre. In some ways, that world is the one all homeless street kids inhabit: a precarious but cunning adaptation to scarce, unpredictable resources. Yet, in another sense, Barrio Libre can exist only on the border. The kids have come here along with everyone else, with or without their families and from as near as Nogales itself or as far as Guadalajara, more than a thousand miles to the south. For them, the border itself and the tunnel underneath it— what better expression of liminality and marginality can one find in the world?—are the very core of their lives. The edge of two nations is their center. They dwell in its ambiguity, irony, contradictions, and subversions.

It is no wonder that the border breeds a kind of consciousness unavailable elsewhere. Perhaps you know where you are only when you are standing at the edge. That is why border people are postmodernists. Even the least reflective among them knows at least that the border is in a sense unreal, an artificiality that can exist only through its constant assertion. The assertion of fences, border patrol, papers, and questions—"American?" "U.S. citizen?" Just as most "white people" don't think about being white, about the cultural creation of a category called "the white race," so, too, Americans and Mexicans may never come to think of "America" and "Mexico" or "American" and "Mexican" as arbitrary ideas that need constant expression to exist. Perhaps they don't need such expression in Iowa or Colima. They do here, though. Living on the border, you may sense that it is not just the "border" that lives only in the will to see it and to act as if it were there, but that Mexico and the United States are also ideas, conspiracies of will and action.

Am I saying that the tunnel kids are philosophers? Most people see them as simply another gang of doped-up, violent, homeless children. Experts often describe them as a collection of pathologies.

I would not underestimate the kids, though. One of their number, El Boston, likes to say, "Every world is a mind, and every mind is a world." This is true for all of them, but in discovering one another's worlds they create a new one that they share.

This book is about that dynamic but fragile, shared world and also about the experiences and conversations through which we entered it. For that entry and sojourn, we of course owe everything to the kids themselves and to house mothers Ramona Encinas and Loida Molina. The staff and board of Mi Nueva Casa allowed and facilitated our work, most especially Claudia Proto, Myrna Ortega, Jan Smith Florez, Dennis Miller, Ron Rosenberg, and Gilbert Rosas. Alberto Comacho was a crucial aid throughout our work. We thank George and Liz Thomson, Kathleen Williamson, and Lisa Otey. We would also like to express our gratitude for the generous support of Lafayette College, Joseph Wilder and the Southwest Center of the University of Arizona, the Arizona Humanities Council, and the School of American Research. Valuable comments on various stages of the project were received from audiences in Nogales, Tucson, the University of Arizona, and the National University of Ireland, Maynooth, as well as from Doug Foley and Martha Sandweiss. Finally, we thank the staff of the University of Arizona Press, particularly our editor, Chris Szuter, our designer Lisa Bowden, and copy editors Annie Barva and Nancy Arora.

The lives of the tunnel kids are disjunctive and fragmentary; so, too, are our knowledge of those lives and, perhaps most of all, our account both of them and of our attempts to understand them. That fragmentary quality may be the condition of all lives and of all human knowledge, but perhaps it is especially so these days and perhaps nowhere more than in places like the Mexico–U.S. border.

Tunnel Kids

t was the morning after the second rains—when I had seen the kids so enjoying life in the tunnel. After several weeks of simply hanging out and chatting with them at Mi Nueva Casa, I had brought the video camera in with me. A couple of the younger boys were there having breakfast and seemed only mildly interested in the camera—a minor diversion from the kung fu films and cartoons. Then the screen door banged open, and El Boston fell in.

At seventeen, he was one of the oldest of the kids, a wary veteran of the streets who had come a long way. Tall and slim, but never starved looking, Boston had a face that was almost Asian, flat and pale olive but with round eyes that flashed and smiled when he wasn't high on paint fumes. He was happiest acting out his *cholo* (street kid) role—striding in great baggy pants, long armless T-shirt, and gleaming "tennies" through the streets of Nogales—or, unselfconsciously slumping on the sofa in Mi Nueva Casa, bouncing Flor's baby, Davidcito, on his lap.

He described himself in a notebook:

El Boston

My name is Pedro
My nickname is El Boston
I am from Guadalajara Tal Mer
I am 17 and live in Nogales, Sonora
I am of Barrio Libre
My birthday is the 3rd of August

I have hung out in the tunnel since I was eleven. When I arrived in Nogales, I had no one, and the situation was very difficult for me since I had absolutely nothing. Then I met a guy from the barrio called Duda who taught me everything, and since then I have had no difficulty getting along in Ambos Nogales. After two months, I returned to my homeland in Guadalajara. I was there nineteen days when my brother came to me and asked if I would take the rails to Nogales. I told him OK, and we went. Afterward, he went off to the south, and I stayed in Tucson, Arizona. Before coming to Nogales, I was a *vato loco*—a "crazy guy of the streets."

So he was still in the eyes of many—a dangerous street thug periodically rounded up with his friends by the Mexican police and by the U.S. Border Patrol when they could catch him. But in his own eyes he was a steady man with responsibilities. Sure, he sniffed spray and smoked *mota* (marijuana), but he was a solid citizen of Barrio Libre, whose hand sign—the fingers arranged in the shape of the letters B and L—he delighted in flashing.

That morning he was looking more ragged than usual. Back in the courtyard behind the kitchen, he threw water on his head from the barrel and smoothed his cholo spikes into neat rows. Satisfied with his toilette, he came into the kitchen, poured a bowl of cornflakes for himself, and then limped over to the table.

"What happened to you?" I asked.

"Oh," he answered, smiling weakly, "I fell."

"In the tunnel?"

"Yeah. I was walking along, and it was dark. We were crossing a group of *pollos* [undocumented immigrants, literally, "chickens"], and I was . . ." He mimed a dizzy, drugged amble, spinning his fingers above his head like the whirling marks above a drunken cartoon character. He laughed again, more heartily, dismissing his own behavior with a wave of the hand.

"And I was arrested this morning."

Too tired and high to make their way back the three miles to a shack in Colonia Los Virreyes, El Boston and his friend Jesús had slept on the projecting cement banks in the tunnel. This preferred place, no doubt because it affords some air and light, is only a few yards in from the American end, *la salida*—the exit. But their drugged sleep had been rudely interrupted by the U.S. Border Patrol. Seeing that I was interested, Boston warmed to his story, although his tone remained matter-of-fact.

"*Migras*—about eight of them—came into the tunnel early in the morning, and they pulled us up from the bench and brought us in. We spent a few hours over there. They took our names and all that information, and then they dumped us back over the line. It's a good thing they didn't check the computer—they would have found me there!"

Boston was blasé. It was a nearly normal morning.

"You have the video again," he noted over his breakfast, looking at the camera on the table. "You filmed us in the tunnel yesterday. Are we going to make a film?"

"We could make a video about all of you here in Mi Nueva Casa," I suggested. "We could go around Nogales and film whatever you think is important. We could start with interviews."

Boston turned serious. "I could do that. ¡*Soy el reportero!*"

"Maybe you could write down some questions to ask all of your friends here," I suggested.

He agreed immediately, and I handed him a piece of paper and a pen. Boston bent to his task. Nose inches from the paper, he scribbled without looking up for half an hour or more. He handed me the completed sheet, a list of numbered, neatly scribed questions, but then took them back before I could read them.

"They are not in the right order. I will recopy them." Finally, Boston handed me his reworked list of forty-four questions (all spelling and grammar errors are in the original):

1. *Como te llamas?* What is your name?
2. *De donde eres?* Where are you from?
3. *Tienes apodo?* Do you have a nickname?
4. *Cual es?* What is it?
5. *Eres de alguno barrio?* Do you belong to any barrio (gang)?
6. *Como se llama?* What is it called?
7. *Te llevas bien con todos?* Do you get along well with everyone?
8. *Con quien te la llevas mejor?* With whom do you get along best?
9. *Usas drogas?* Do you use drugs?
10. *Cuales drogas usas?* Which drugs do you use?
11. *Donde esta ese barrio?* Where is this barrio?
12. *Son muchos?* Are there many (in the barrio)?
13. *Que hacen en tu barrio?* What do they do in your barrio?
14. *Has tenido broncas con los de tu barrio o con otros de otro barrio?* Have you had fights with others in your barrio or with those of another barrio?
15. *Tienes mucho tiempo en ese barrio?* Have you been in your barrio for a long time?
16. *Cuanto tiempo, mas o menos?* How long, more or less?
17. *Nunca te as aburrido de tu barrio?* Have you ever been bored, fed up, with your barrio?
18. *Por que?* Why?
19. *Tienen armas en tu barrio?* Do they have weapons in your barrio?
20. *Te gusta ser cholo de tu barrio?* Do you like being a cholo of your barrio?
21. *Por que?* Why?
22. *Has pensado en cambiar de personalidad?* Have you ever thought of changing your personality? Your self?
23. *Si tu fueras el rey de este mundo te gustaria que ubieran cholos?* If you were king of this world, would you like there to be cholos?
24. *Por que?* Why?
25. *Eres feliz como eres?* Are you happy as you are?
26. *Por que?* Why?

27. *Has estado en peligro de muerte alguna vez?* Have you ever been in danger of death?
28. *En que forma?* In what form?
29. *Siempre te has vestido como cholo?* Have you always dressed as a cholo?
30. *A los cuantos años entraste a tu barrio?* At what age did you enter your barrio?
31. *Antes de entrar te gustaban las drogas?* Before entering, did you like drugs?
32. *Siempre has estado en este barrio?* Have you always been in this barrio?
33. *Por que le pusieron así ó quien le puso así?* What or who got you into it?
34. *Estudias ó trabajas?* Do you study or work?
35. *Tienes novia?* Do you have a girlfriend?
36. *Quien es ella, es bonita?* Who is she, is she pretty?
37. *Es de tu barrio ó de otro barrio ó es decente?* Is she from your barrio, another barrio, or is she decent?
38. *Como se llama?* What's her name?
39. *Ella te quiere?* Does she love you?
40. *Le gustas?* Do you like her?
41. *Te llevas bien con su familia y tambien con ella?* Do you get along well with her family and with her as well?
42. *Cuantos años tienes?* How old are you?
43. *Y ella?* And she?
44. *Piensas casarte con ella?* Do you think about getting married to her?

Reading through these questions, I was stunned by their number and surprised by their direction. They began as you might expect: "What's your name? Where are you from?" But the subsequent questions sought nothing more on the distant past of family and *tierra* (homeland), turning rather to where and how the kids lived and who they were now—in and under the streets of Nogales. Boston wanted to explore the life of Barrio Libre. The markers of that life, of that identity, were clear in the questions: fights, drugs, and clothes. Most of all, he wanted to know how long and how deep was their sense of belonging in that fellowship.

But then, somewhere in middle of the list, Boston's focus switched. Subtly, his questions began to suggest a certain ambivalence: he wanted to press his friends to defend their life and even to think about the future.

> Have you ever been bored by your barrio?
> Why?
> Have you thought of changing your way of being?
> If you were king of this world, would you like there to be cholos?
> Why?
> Are you happy as you are?
> Why?

The intent seemed almost subversive—and from Boston, the most cholo of cholos. Further down the list, he returned to the life of the barrio, but in a more reflective and even critical way that might encourage his friends to think about how they had been changed, and not always for the better, since joining the gang. That same mood seemed to continue with questions that linked the present with the future: questions about girlfriends and boyfriends and about the possibility of marriage.

"Very interesting," I said. "Do you want to ask them something more about the future at the end? Like where they hope to be, say, ten years from now?" Boston liked the idea, but tempered the "hope." He wrote, *"Dentro de diez años mas adelante, que cres que pase contigo?"*—"In another ten years, what do you believe will be happening with you?"

Those were Boston's questions.

I was evidently impressed, and he was proud, but all business. "Let's go in the schoolroom," he told me. "I will interview everyone, and you can film it with the video camera."

"Juán," he announced to one of his friends, "come with us; you're first."

And so he began his interviews. His friends were made to file in one by one. Some were laughing—thinking the whole exercise a joke; others were nervous or truculent and gave only one-word answers.

Why do they like the life of Barrio Libre? Because they are free, because they party together.

Boston, through it all, maintained a seriousness of purpose and decorum that amazed me. He was insistent. If someone was making noise in the next room, he told him to shut up. He wrote down every answer, and if someone seemed disinclined to address a question, he cajoled and offered possible responses. Nearly everyone seemed as surprised as I was by the questions probing their attachment to their way of life: "Are they happy as they are?" "If they were king of this world, . . . ?"

Many received these questions with visible discomfort, answering "sure" without obvious conviction, but a few took the opportunity to say something quietly to themselves: "Yes, there should be cholos, but without the violence." Or even, "No, because there is too much violence." I couldn't be sure, but such answers seemed not at all directed to my presence in the corner. They were muttered almost below earshot.

They had the greatest difficulty with my own question concerning the future. Where would they be ten years down the road? Chito said he would change at eighteen. Flor said that she couldn't even say what would be happening to her tomorrow, much less that far ahead. Most of them simply stared in silence. The question might as well have asked what they would be doing fifty years in the future. At the end of each interview, as if to contradict any sense that he meant to undermine their faith in Barrio Libre, Boston had each of them flash the sign of the barrio for the video camera.

It was late in the afternoon, and Boston had slowly questioned five of his friends. I thought that he must be tired of it.

"Is that enough?" I asked him.

"When you do interviews," he replied, "which is better, many or few?" He did not need to wait for the answer. "We'll do them today, tomorrow, and Friday, then we will go out into the streets."

We continued for two more days, with Boston writing down every

Mike

answer on the sheets of questions that I had photocopied—as he had asked.

No doubt, many social scientists would maintain that Boston's interviews yielded little reliable data, but this story is not about survey questionnaires. It is about questions: whose they are, where they come from, and where they are going. In fact, most ethnographic fieldwork consists of neither questionnaires nor surveys, nor even of interviews, but rather of conversations. Clearly, Boston's writing of the questions and the event of the interviews themselves were important moments in what we might call an ongoing conversation between Boston and me, but also between Boston and his friends, and, perhaps most of all, between Boston and himself.

I say "conversation," but I do not wish to convey any illusion that our positions and power were equal. Both Boston and I had our goals, however—goals that dovetailed enough for one protracted moment in which something fruitful, even revelatory, could happen. I had a loose and patient agenda: simply to find out something about their lives. Boston decided to seize the moment by assuming a role my presence and behavior allowed and facilitated. It was the only way, perhaps, that he could have asked his questions. He could not have said to his friends, "Let's pretend I am a reporter asking you questions." He could not have said that even to himself. But clearly, Boston had questions to ask—or he did as soon as he thought about it.

I asked him to write the questions down beforehand because I wanted him to think. I was hoping that Boston might like to write. Maeve was beginning to teach some of the kids how to use a camera, and I was thinking that maybe someone like Boston could more easily find his own thoughts with the aid of a pen. We were told that these kids—so drugged and damaged as they were by their lives and by the paint fumes they sniffed—had attention spans of perhaps ten minutes and learning abilities of kids less than half their ages. We were already doubting these assumptions before the episode of the questions. If these kids were stupid, if they could not learn, they would be dead.

But, even so, I was not prepared for the complexity of thought revealed by Boston's questions. They were a guide to the kids' view of their own lives and culture; they revealed as well a degree of self-consciousness, of awareness that they were caught in a kind of performance. In formulating and then asking the questions, Boston not only had seized the moment, but had taken over our conversation. I was thinking that if he was willing to say so much, the others might be, too, and I should be willing to listen. There was always a chance I might learn something.

On Friday afternoon, the interviews were over, and Boston and I were out in the courtyard of Mi Nueva Casa, talking about life on the streets. He liked the idea of using the video camera to film their lives and asked whether he could see the film I had made of them playing in the tunnel, kicking the ball around. I found the tape, and we watched it on the little camera screen. Boston laughed at the sight of his girlfriend, La Negra, falling hysterically into the churning waters.

"Remember, Lorenzo, when we asked you to get us some food?" he asked, suddenly serious, even teacherly. I did remember. They had not shown up at Mi Nueva Casa that day and so had not eaten there. The directors had complained that they must be induced to come in, and I thought—when they asked me to throw snacks down to them—that I should instead tell them to go to the Casa for a meal. So I did. But that decision was not playing by their rules, and I knew it at the time. I also knew that it was a kind of test to see where I really fit in—a test that I had failed. Now Boston was giving me another chance.

"You always give food like that. You should have got, maybe, a couple of bags of chips and thrown them down to us. That is how we are." I nodded, thinking that this choice was only one—and a relatively easy one—among many that I might face between following their rules or those of Mi Nueva Casa and the world it represented.

Then Boston wanted to see something of his interviews, and I popped another cassette in the camera. He listened and watched intently.

"Your questions were interesting, Boston. What did you think of them yourself?" I asked when we were finished watching.

"I made these questions thinking about who likes being a cholo, more or less," he answered, "and to get their names and tierra, so that you could know who they are and where they are from. But the questions about *el barrio* are to see who really follows the way of the barrio and who does not; who likes it and who does not. Questions like 'If you were king of this world . . .' made them think. Made them think, well, about who likes being a cholo, more or less. But I didn't ask difficult questions. I asked simple questions so that they could answer. They take so much paint, it makes them crazy, and they can't think straight."

"What do you think about their answers?" I asked.

"Sometimes, two or three of them said to me that they were going to tell lies. I said to them, 'You can answer the way you want; in any case, it is you who will lie, not me. Anyway, this isn't for the government; it's for us.'"

He continued, "Have you ever heard it said that 'every world is a mind, every mind is a world,' if you understand me? For example, I don't know what you think of us, you don't know what I think of you, or what the others think of you, or what anybody thinks of all this, see? Probably many of them were telling me lies, nothing more, to seem OK. And as for me, sometimes I am confused, and I am looking at them, but I am not really paying attention. You may be talking to me, and I might be nodding like I am listening, but maybe I am only looking, not really hearing."

He paused and then continued with what only appeared to be a non sequitur.

"But what is important to me is what is going to happen tomorrow. I say that with luck I will change. Anyway, I would like there to be a counselor to talk with us and ask us questions about what we think of the barrio. And we should answer him sincerely. And he would tell us that our lives are like that for such and such reason. The others think that such people are all with the government, and when they take photos of them, they are scared. But I would really like someone to come here, a counselor, a good one. He would ask questions to see what they would do in the future, and that would make them think, 'I don't have studies; I don't have the means to become anything.' So they would reason, and they would know that it's good to get out of their crazy lives for a little while. That they should change. And that they should respect someone's decision to change and not say, 'Look, it's stupid to go and change, ugh' because they want to stop him."

"If tomorrow I say that I want to change," he continued, getting closer to his own feelings perhaps, "they should not say to me, 'Look, what is this change business?' because that way, how am I going to succeed? If I say I am going to change, maybe the other guys feel offended. But if I keep up this life of vice, I am going to be all fucked up. Maybe I seem happy. But the happiness passes, and I am going to want to attack someone. So there comes a time when you have to do it, you have to change."

Writing down that conversation later, I realized that this talk about a counselor who, with the right questions, could have helped Boston and the others find a way out may have been directed at both me and himself. Maybe he hoped that I would help him to change. Maybe if I had asked the right question. "Every mind is a world . . ."

Even if Boston had other motives for cooperating with me, saying what he figured I wanted to hear with the hope of some as yet undiscovered return, he in fact got little out of the relationship—except, I like to believe, a chance to think and to hang out with an older male who appeared to care about him. As for me, it was the beginning of a long conversation, first with Boston but increasingly with the others of Barrio Libre.

P one *La Poderosa*," Chito "of the flood" said, leaning from the back seat toward the radio dial. Jesús, who was next to me, more angling than pointing my video camera out the window, found their favorite station—La Poderosa, the "Powerful One"—and Los Tigres del Norte began to sing "El mojado acaudalado" or "The Wealthy Wetback." Everyone in the car belted out the lyrics. Even La Flor's baby, Davidcito, seemed to gurgle along with the music, which provided a backbeat for the cacophony of the streets as we jerked up Avenida Obregón, past the last tourist markets and into the jumble of tiny shops, gas stations, and swarming people. It is no wonder the kids like video games, I thought, as I negotiated the unpredictable perils of veering cars and lurching pedestrians. I was still making the novice's mistake of obeying stop signs and thus confusing everyone coming into the intersection. The key, I eventually discovered, is to keep moving because everybody is timing his movements accordingly. To stop is to cause confusion, consternation, and havoc.

So we bumped along over the gaping potholes, through clouds of desert dust or flooded side streets, with a running commentary from all the kids, as proud as Paris tour guides. La Flor was in the back, next to Chito and Boston, quietly bouncing Davidcito on her lap. Jesús was leaning out the window, shouting and flashing Barrio Libre signs at the dozens of street kids he knew, all the while filming at drunken angles. Everyone was shouting directions, "Left here, right there, up here—don't worry, you can make it. Drive!"

These particular kids formed a kind of family within Barrio Libre and the strongest link between the world of the streets and Mi Nueva Casa. At the center, however quiet, were little Flor, a soft, delicate girl of fifteen, and her six-month old baby boy, Davidcito. He was the child of her previous boyfriend, but she had been with Jesús since soon after his birth. At the Casa, they were often together on the battered sofa, with Davidcito on one lap or the other. Flor said little, but the short, flat-faced, and occasionally boisterous Jesús looked and acted like a Mexican version of *Angels with Dirty Faces*. Chito and Boston were their closest friends, and Boston in particular took an avuncular interest in the little family, often sweeping Davidcito up into his arms as he passed by. So when Boston had suggested an excursion, the others came along. For me, it was the first of many of our drives and walks together through Nogales, Sonora, the chaotic, ruckus, border city that was home to these kids and that I was beginning to see through their eyes. I knew it as dirty, colorful, and jumping with life. They found it ugly but exciting: a place of many opportunities, dangers, and even memories.

We passed first through the older part of Nogales, a narrow grid of *avenidas* and *calles* about a mile and a half in length and one-third as wide. The steeply rising hills to the east and west were covered with housing of every description, though most were jerry-rigged shacks of plywood or even cardboard. Though the word *"colonias"* actually applies to any urban subdistrict—rich or poor, old or new—in its generic usage it had come to mean only these sprawling slums.

The new *periférico* (bypass road) circled the town, bringing the constant stream of trucks loaded with Mexican produce across the border at a new gate about a mile west of city center. The train, however, still passed across the border right in the middle of town, where a heavy metal gate slid away to let it through, but slowly enough so

La Flor and Davidcito

that a dozen U.S. Border Patrol agents could search it for stowaways. Here at the border gates, downtown Nogales, Arizona, met downtown Nogales, Sonora. A multilane car crossing was jammed with traffic at morning and afternoon rush hours, but a small army of vendors took advantage of that captive audience to hawk their goods—from sacks of home-made dried beef to pirate cassettes to huge plaster statues of Crucified Jesus or Smiling Tweety-birds and Bart Simpsons. Most of the cars were driven by either Mexicans or Mexican Americans who lived on one side and worked on the other. Each of them was interrogated by customs officials, who sent one of every few vehicles into an inspection bay to be sniffed by dogs and subjected to anything from a cursory once-over to total disassembly. The drug busts were regular and occasionally dramatic; that same week, a driver had panicked at the gate, leaped from his car, and dashed back into Mexico. They did not catch him, but they had found twenty-three million dollars worth of cocaine in the car. A great deal more was probably getting through without trouble, not only in cars, but also under the border by means of the tunnels.

On the U.S. side of the line, a few fast food restaurants and many shops were selling basic consumer items—groceries, cheap electronics, and assorted dry goods—to far fewer Mexican shoppers than in the days of a stronger peso. The Mexican side was much more crowded and included several streets of tourist shops, dozens of little groceries, eateries, *farmacias,* and both decent and many smaller, seedier hotels.

The streets were filled with three kinds of people: American shoppers seeking tourist trinkets, discount dentists, or cheap prescriptions at the farmacias; the poor from elsewhere in Mexico and countries farther south; and those locals who lived off one or both of these groups of outsiders. But the locals, too, were often enough recent migrants from farther to the south. Since the late 1970s, the city had grown from thirty thousand to more than two hundred thousand—though no one seemed to have anything more than a very approximate idea of their numbers. Although some Americans stayed overnight, the vast majority walked across the border, spent a few hours shopping, perhaps having a meal in one of four or five restaurants that looked familiar enough to risk, and then walked back to their cars parked in the United States. The poor Mexicans from the south were to be found in sorry crowds in and around the seedy hotels, where they paid high rates while waiting for their *pollero* or *coyote* (people smuggler) to take them across the border. They milled around in the lobbies and *taquerías,* and lined up outside at the pay phone from which they could call family members already in the United States to arrange their arrival.

"Turn here," Chito said into my ear, "I will show you where I first slept in Nogales and where I met Jesús." We bounced over the railroad tracks and headed along the border fence. In taking me to this place, Chito was continuing the conversation we had begun the day before at Mi Nueva Casa just after Boston's interviews.

Remembering that Boston's questions included one about where they were from, I had asked Chito about his native city, Navojoa, several hundred miles into Mexico, in the southern part of the large border state of Sonora. Chito had smiled over the Formica table, conjuring the scene he had left.

"It's beautiful there. Much prettier than other places I have been, like Ciudad Juárez. I spent a few months there with an aunt and cousin, working in a small store she had there. That was an ugly place. But other places in Chihuahua are better, like San Benito and San Rafael. I was in all those places, even down in El Fuerte in Sinaloa."

Well traveled for a boy of fifteen, I thought, but appearing unlikely for the role. Chito had the delicacy and pallor of a rabbinical student; it was difficult to picture him having lived years on the street, much less in the tunnel.

"Shall I tell you the story of when I was little?" he had continued. "What can I tell you? My mom had me in 1981. She had a taco stand; she still has it. But she couldn't take care of me, and I was raised by Grandmother. She died when I was eleven, but I still lived there. I used to wash cars, and I met a bus driver. He asked me, 'Do you want to go with me?' I used to eat with him. I washed the windows of all of the buses, and he said I could stay there to take care of the buses. I used to sleep there, and in the morning I would get money from him.

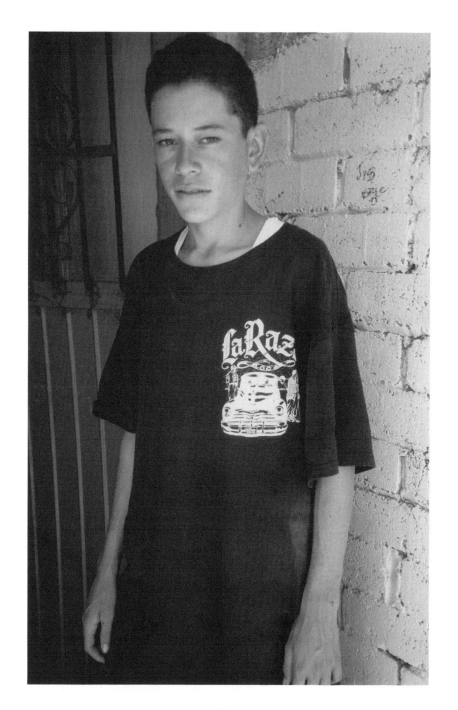

Chito

But I didn't like it, and I came here. Well, I really did like it . . . but another kid used to go with me, and some stereos got stolen, and maybe they blamed me. But the owner said, 'No, you are all right, you stay here; stay here and wash the buses.'

"But I left. I came to Nogales because I like this place. Navojoa, I didn't like. I don't know why. I don't like my relatives, gossiping around, controlling me. When I go there, I don't get involved with them. I go see my mom and my brothers, and then come back. My father died a year and a half ago.

"How did I come here? I got paid and bought the train ticket. It costs seventy-two pesos for the train, to come here, so I got one hundred and fifty for the ticket and for food. Now when I go back, I give my mother money, and she takes care of it, and when I ask, she gives it to me. The last time I came here it was with four others from Navojoa, and now I do it myself. My cousin Billy is here in Nogales and friends came, too. But they went back to Navojoa and don't come any more."

I had asked him what he wanted to do with his life, and he had answered without hesitation.

"*Camionero.*" Bus driver. "I have a friend—the man who took care of me in Navojoa. He is the owner of the bus route, and I will get work with him in Navojoa when I am eighteen." He had leaned over the table with great excitement. "He drives a bus, and he lets me go with him, sit beside him, as he drives around; sometimes I take the money from the people, and I sit beside him. And then at the end of the day or if there are no passengers, he lets me drive!"

He had imitated the bumping motion of a heavy bus jolting violently with every gear change, his eyes aflame with humor and determined desire.

"Then later I would do it better," and he had mimed a smoother drive, a chugging glide up the hill. "They don't use first gear, only second, because they are so *poderoso*."

That had been the day before our drive, and Chito now wanted to take me to one of his *lieux de mémoire*. My own car was not so poderoso, and I wondered if it would make it to wherever he was taking us. We turned to the west right at the solid steel border fence, following Calle Internacional to the foot of a very steep hill, and parked at the dead end of a side street. We all followed Chito on foot up a set of broken concrete stairs that perhaps had once led to a house but now brought us to the edge of a small field of stones and desert grass, covered with the debris of the surrounding homes.

"This," Chito said, with a slow look around at the terraced hillsides covered with houses, dogs, and children, "is Buenos Aires." All the colonias had names like that. From where we stood, we could easily see the border fence perhaps a hundred yards to the north. Because of its proximity to *la línea* and its twisted, gully passages and hidden heights and perches, Buenos Aires was a dangerous place. I remembered my first visit three years earlier. We had watched several men usher a long line of immigrants through a large hole they had snipped in the fence, a few hundred yards up the steep slope, while four or five Mexican policemen chatted at the bottom of the hill as local kids washed their cars. A tranquil border scene with everyone doing his job, disturbed only by a burst of automatic gunfire somewhere farther up the colonia paths, sending would-be Americans scurrying for shelter and the police, more than reluctantly, on a slow walk up the hill in the direction of the fire.

"This is where I slept when I first came to Nogales," Chito said, pointing to a twisted little mesquite in the middle of a field of broken glass. The door of a Chevrolet had been dragged over and propped up near the tree to provide the illusion of shelter. A depressing first night, I could not help thinking. But, as Chito told me, he was not alone; other street kids had in fact directed him to this place.

"And here," Chito continued, "I met Jesús."

Jesús smiled sweetly, standing on the spot where they first met.

"Jesús told me about Barrio Libre, and so I joined. We slept here for a few months. Usually it was OK, but then it got too cold."

"There is an entrance to the tunnel—Los Vampiros—just over there, but it is too hot today," referring to the danger, not the temperature. "But we can go to the other one." So we left the field of broken glass and dreams, and headed south, away from the border through the teeming streets. After about a mile, we pulled over next to a tree-lined crossroads, and I followed them on foot again, over a wall and down into a big wash running right through the middle of the city. The wide, deeply rutted dirt bottom was dry at the time and led under the road on which we had been traveling. Once under the overpass, we found ourselves in a cavernous passage leading to the tunnel. Inside was cool and dank, pervaded by the smell of urine and excrement. The walls were covered with graffiti.

"*Aquí está mi placaso,*" Jesús told me, pointing to a great looping signature in black—his calling card. Beneath it, more flowing script in the same color paint—*La Flor*. Their names were two of dozens—an incredible collage of words and signs that covered every inch of the walls and disappeared into the darkness. In less than one hundred feet, the passage met the tunnel proper, which ran north to the border. We all sat on a concrete ledge, looking in that direction.

"There is always water in this one," Flor explained. As my eyes began to adjust enough to make out the inky ribbon beneath us, Boston spoke, his quiet voice nearly echoing in the cool dank.

"We are sometimes here, but more often we go to the other one, the dry one [tunnel]. We take *pollos* through. Sometimes we do it ourselves. We charge them three hundred pesos and take them across to the other side. And sometimes we work with the coyotes, the polleros. We might be lookouts, help them get the pollos through."

"Do you rob them, then, the pollos?" I asked.

Boston smiled almost shyly. "Yes. Well, we ask them—*los chuntaros* [scrawny, dumb people of no worth] we call them—to give us money. We demand it, and they give it."

I knew they took more than money because immigrants were regularly emerging from the U.S. side of the tunnel not only broke but also naked. I could not help thinking that these same victims were just like the kids' own families. The kids could easily be robbing and terrorizing their own cousins or neighbors. I said as much, asking if they felt at all bad about that.

"No, no, you don't understand," Jesús said. "These pollos are not Mexicans; they are from other countries—from Guatemala, Nicaragua, like that." And to confirm the point, he opened a worn wallet and took out a Guatemalan currency note, which I inspected as Boston continued.

"That's right. The ones we rob are from those other places; many are from El Salvador. We don't bother Mexicans. They tell us that they are Mexicans, but we know from the way they talk that they are not. Anyway, I have seen these people—these Salvadorans—in Tucson. Have you? Well they are like animals. They are terrible people."

I wondered if everyone needed to feel that way about some group of people. I was also thinking about the polleros and the coyotes. Even if the kids worked together with them sometimes, wouldn't they also be competitors by running their own underground railroad? I asked, and Boston replied, "No, we can get along, mostly we get along with the polleros. We will help them, and they know they can count on us. And they look away; they leave us to do what we do."

But I remembered Boston's question about their being in danger of death. One of the kids, Juanito, had referred to an incident with a coyote, who had slugged him with a pistol and then jammed it in his face.

"Yeah," said Boston. "Sometimes there can be trouble. Like, if he feels maybe you have gone too far—'passed the point of being a prick.' That's what they'll say to you."

We filed silently out of the tunnel and climbed back to the road, where clouds of barbecued chicken smoke purged the stench from my nose if not my mind. A short drive and we came to a small park wedged between the wide and traffic-choked avenidas.

"That," Boston remarked, pointing out the window toward a massive, towering bronze statue in the socialist-realist style, "is El Mono Vichi"—the Stupid or Naked Dummy. "Here we wash windshields," Chito said. I pulled over to the curb, and sure enough, when the light turned red at the intersection under the statue, about a half a dozen boys—a few as young as ten or eleven—leaped into the street, plastic water spray bottle, filthy rag, and wiper in hands. They rushed to the front few cars and began to wash their windows. The drivers either stared straight ahead or, more often, gestured negatively with a shaking finger. But unless the rejection was very emphatic, the kids continued to wash. If the driver seemed agreeable, they would take the time to do as good a job as possible, flicking and flourishing their rags with style and pride. In any case, as Chito explained, some pay and some don't. "We get anything from a couple of pesos to a few dollars—from Americans. They're the best."

Chito whistled out the window, and the kids saw him and ran over to us. Two of them furiously washed the windshield while the others thrust ecstatic and curious faces into the car, slapping hands with everyone inside. Chito was the closest to this crowd, and he quickly gathered intelligence: "Who has been here and for how long, how much was taken in, any hassles?" Jesús sauntered back to the car—I hadn't seen him get out—with *paletas,* frozen fruit bars, for everyone, including the little window washer kids.

Soon we were on the road again, heading farther south. As we approached the edge of the city, the vista widened, and newly plowed, wide dirt roads led into industrial parks with dozens of huge, hangerlike structures. *"Maquiladoras,"* Boston said. "There are many of them." In fact, there were nearly one hundred by then, assembly plants that formed the core of the new industry dominating every big Mexican border town and a fair few some distance into the interior.

"There, turn left," Boston told me, and we jolted over the railroad tracks that, like the main road here, traveled from south to north, from the rest of Mexico to the border. We sailed through a knot of cars nudging one another in a triple dirt-road intersection and began to climb slowly out of the narrow valley floor of the city and up increasingly provisional and crumbling roads into the colonias that housed the great majority of Nogalenses.

"Here is Solidaridad. I know those people there," Jesús said, nodding toward a knot of young men, women, and dust-smeared, lively children chatting by a large white plastic pipe jutting out of a dirt hillside. Behind them were a ditch road and a line of houses, each assembled out of available materials—particle board, plywood, cardboard, even sheets of plastic—fastened together and topped by roofs of yet more uncertain construction, considering the sudden winds and rains of the summer storms. The sheets of tar paper or tin were weighted down by concrete blocks or large stones—or, in one fascinating case, by all the metal belongings of the family, including several bicycles and a wheelbarrow.

From the open car window, Jesús was waving at and filming the laughing crowd. When I pulled over, he popped out to delight the children by recording their antics and then playing the tape for them. Meanwhile, the adults by the pipe explained that this source of water for the hundreds of people who lived in the neighborhood had been dry for several days. Though they smiled and laughed as they spoke, they told us that they had just returned from a massive demonstration at the city hall. Several thousand from a few of the colonias on this side of the city were similarly afflicted, and a mob of angry protestors had confronted the indifference of official Nogales.

"They treat us like shit," a young man said, but several of the young women seemed hopeful that their protests would bring some change. If nothing else, their common plight had brought some of them together, a bit of "solidarity" after all—a good thing in a neighborhood to which people had come only recently from many other parts of Mexico and where they hence often knew little of each other: a poor world made twice dangerous, for it is far easier to rob or hurt a stranger. We wished them luck and climbed back into the car to continue on our way to the *casita* where, as Jesús had told me, all the kids had been sleeping for some months.

We weren't more than a hundred yards beyond the dry pipe, though, when I saw a police car—or rather pickup truck—in the rearview mirror, its light flashing. The kids, of course, had already noted it and told me to pull over. They didn't seem worried, but I certainly was as I turned my head to see two *municipales*—city police officers—walking up to either side of the car, hands draped lazily on their still-holstered revolvers. One looked inside. I couldn't see the cop's eyes behind his sunglasses, but he seemed relaxed, leaning in through the window and taking in the strange mix of passengers. "Where are you going?" he asked, his tone only slightly betraying what he was probably thinking—that there was nowhere in the vicinity I should have been going.

"I am working at Mi Nueva Casa," I explained, "helping these kids." Boston, always the slickest, added in his best we-are-grateful-to-be-helped voice, "He is a volunteer, a counselor; he takes us places and teaches us things." Just the opposite, I thought, but the cops seemed satisfied, and they ambled back to the truck and pulled out ahead of us, sending up a wake of dust. Before we had driven more than half a mile, we saw them again. This time they pulled up behind a battered local truck and got out carefully, walking slowly toward the truck with automatic rifles pointed before them.

I realized that the kids were more than familiar with being stopped by the police and with watching their armed antics. One of the many contradictions of the border is that the Mexican government is both weak and ever present. "Poor Nogales, so far from Mexico City, so close to the United States," to paraphrase the famous expression. The very distance from the center makes the presence of the state more obvious, more intrusive in the border towns than perhaps anywhere in Mexico. The number of armed, uniformed— however informally—men in the streets is stunning. Thinking back, I realized that we had seen no fewer than five different police forces that day. There were the two khaki-suited municipales that had just stopped us. Patrolling the border had been the black T-shirt-wearing, swaggering elite Betas. The Sonoran and Special Highway Police had been cruising the main avenida. A carload of *fiscales* (part of a federal force in charge of monetary matters) had been parked somewhere downtown. Last, but most showy, was the open-back truckload of heavily armed *federales,* infamous from song and motion picture, that had passed us, careering through the downtown streets. As the headlines in the local paper constantly reveal, those various forces act more or less like the armies of warlords, openly resenting one another and sometimes dangerously close to armed confrontation.

These bands of armed enforcers, I was beginning to realize, were a crucial feature of the local world for these kids, however nonchalant they seemed at the moment. So many police, any of whom might at any moment decide to sweep up any number of them—"the usual suspects"—and throw them in the rat's hole of a city jail for a few days. From there, they could be sent for a longer stay in the more commodious juvenile detention facility on the edge of the city. When we had passed that place earlier in the excursion, Jesús had pointed the video camera toward it, and they had all shouted out how many months they had spent there.

El Boston, who must have been brooding since our visit to Chito's field, suddenly spoke up with some determination. "Do you want to see where I first slept in Nogales?" But before I could answer, he continued, "Go right here." We began a descent out of Colonia Solidaridad and through the older, more traditionally ramshackle neighborhoods that clustered around the railroad station. We parked in front of the station, which has to be one of the largest and ugliest buildings in Nogales—a cavernous modern concrete shell, already streaked and cracked everywhere, with huge panes of broken and taped glass that magnify the sun's intensity until it feels like a blistering, suffocating blanket. We all piled out of the car and followed Boston beyond the station to a line of graffiti-covered boxcars that looked as if they had sat disabled on these tracks for decades.

"Here," Boston said, pointing to one of them, "was where I began my life in Nogales." He was smirking, but serious, even a little proud. We all gathered around to listen, La Flor softly jostling Davidcito in her arms.

"I arrived in the station and wandered around. This guy came up to me, an older guy, and I guess he saw I was a stranger and knew absolutely nothing—*nada de nada*. 'Come here,' he said to me. 'You need a place to stay? You can stay over there in the boxcars; no one will bother you.' So I followed him to this place, and here I spent my first nights in Nogales. It was crazy; all kinds of things went on in the cars. Everyone was stoned. People screwed. Well, then sometime a little later, I met Duda—like I told you—and he took me to another place where *cholos* of the Barrio were staying, and I stayed there with them."

I looked nervously around at the apparently deserted railroad cars, but the scene was already changing, and a few heads appeared sleepily around corners, looking at us with less curiosity than I expected. Chito in particular was surveying the scene, taking in everything.

Throughout the tour, La Flor had been saying very little indeed, yet she was clearly enjoying herself, happy to be part of this excursion and smiling with a look of self-confidence and security that I had never seen on her face at Mi Nueva Casa. It was as if she were looking at her own family album.

"Let's go to the casita," said Jesús. "It's only just up there." And so we were off again, taking small lanes through the railroad yards and surrounding neighborhoods.

"Right," Jesús said, and we turned up a nearly vertical path that looked far less like a road than a dry riverbed, deeply gullied and strewn with stones. At the top was an equally rough but horizontal patch of dirt, parking for Jesús' casita. "This is it," he said, "come."

So this, I thought, was the other "home"—the flip side of Mi Nueva Casa and, of course, its inversion in many ways. It was a simple square shack made up of sheets of plywood nailed onto a frame of two-by-fours, the whole thing covered with tar paper. There were two tiny windows and an open doorway. The adults at Mi Nueva Casa called it the *cascarón*—the eggshell. Rough enough, but I had already seen worse. A few yards away stood the outhouse, a circle of upright poles woven with lengths of burlap, the loose ends flapping like ensigns in the breeze. Many other houses surrounded us, all of them more substantial. The one closest above was just a shell of bricks, but already looking more habitable than the casita. A small Catholic Church of cinder blocks was under construction just beyond. I could not help thinking that the neighbors must have been wishing that this shack full of cholos would blow off the hill.

As we approached the casita, Guanatos stepped out of the gloom, squinting into the afternoon sun. Tall, slim, and dark, Guanatos, like Boston, was from Guadalajara. Even in his dirt-streaked T-shirt, sleepy-eyed from drugs, he was lithe and elegant. With an exaggerated sweep of his arm and a half bow, he invited me in: *"Mi casa es su casa."* My eyes adjusted slowly to the dark, at first discerning only the faces and white shirts of kids on the floor. After a few moments, I could see a dirt floor, hard from months of trodding, a collapsing iron bed with a thin mattress, and an assortment of bedding strewn on the floor. Guanatos took little Davidcito from La Flor's arms and, softly bouncing and cooing, carried him to whoever was inside for their admiration. I found a vinyl car seat in the corner, and we all settled down for the moment.

Jesús explained, "This belongs to a brother of my mother, and so we can stay here. It's not too bad." But Guanatos, who was sitting

Guanatos

beside me, leaned over and said, *"Hay nada—nada de nada."* There's nothing, absolutely nothing. I could then clearly make out the others there. Across from me was the other, much darker Jesús, who was called Negro, and his sister, Boston's girlfriend, Negra—Judith. I knew them from Mi Nueva Casa, where Negro was typically expressionless and slow with fatigue. Here he was quicker but naturally guarded, surprised at my entrance into this world. As for Negra, she was the opposite of Flor, happy on the surface but mercurial and explosive. She played like a girl far younger than her thirteen years, falling hysterically into mud and water in the tunnel, but did not hesitate to whip out a knife if she felt provoked. The ladies at Mi Nueva Casa considered her a very bad lot. A few days before, she had been tossed out of the Casa for another burst of typically disruptive behavior; angry over something, she had given Flor's hair a good yank and sent her sprawling on the floor. Since then she had been hanging out across the street from Mi Nueva Casa when the kids were inside. Boston would smuggle out her lunch. I could not help liking her. There was something appealing to me in her eye-flashing spirit, and maybe she needed to be wild to survive, for like the other girls she had had much to contend with—not only the usual perils of the life in the streets, but tricks turned with truckers in a sleazy border dive, the Hotel Miami, a line of work she had begun at twelve. "She is a wild one," Boston had already told me. "No one can control her." He had doubts about their future together.

Maybe it was because we were sheltered from the last blasts of the desert sun in a dirt-floored hut, but I began to see these kids as less like a gang—at least as gangs are normally described—than like a clan of hunter-gatherers. Like the !Kung of the Kalahari Desert or Eskimos in the arctic, they were finding a way to survive in a particularly harsh environment. As with those other hardy bands, they found or built shelter, scouted out the resources, and watched for the many perils of the world around them.

But, of course, this world was less a creation of nature than the often awful artifact of national and global forces that combined and collided to create the border in all its power and ambiguity. That line emphatically divided, blocked, frustrated—even as it connected,

Gerónimo

drew, seduced. A flow of goods and people passed across and under it: the inexorable tides of international capital and human hunger for a better life or the chemical means to escape this one. The Mexican and U.S. governments played at the game of encouraging or defeating this flow, even as everyone, from multinational corporate executives and generals to these poor kids, scurried to profit from it whatever he or she could.

All of which made the "environment" to which the kids had to adapt far more shifting, unstable, and unpredictable than the Kalahari or the Arctic. The sources of food, cash, favors, and so on were here today, gone tomorrow. The tunnel in which they had "foraged" yesterday was "too hot" today, patrolled by the hated Grupo Beta. And the same coyote who had been their friend, who had given them some pesos for acting as lookouts at *la salida del túnel* (tunnel exit), now drew a pistol, told them that they had gone too far—"passed the point of being a prick" in the local idiom—and fired a warning shot into one's leg.

In such a world, survival required two crucial ingredients: possessing knowledge and being part of a group that could be trusted. They had to know all they could of the ever-changing scene, where, at any given moment, good things were to be had and grim dangers avoided. The kids had been showing me both features of their lives all day. They had taken me through their world—pointing out the places where they found food or money or where their enemies lurked. They had also been seizing every opportunity to gather intelligence, to find out whatever they could of everyone's movements and of the shifting shape of friends and enemies. They had also retraced their own local histories, reenacting their lonely arrivals and the ways in which they had found each other and Barrio Libre. The outing had, once again, reconfirmed their collective understanding, showing that they had a common history, shared memories—memories that sometimes softened and deepened the city for them. In fact, our excursion soon became part of that shared past, for in the months that followed they would often refer to it, saying, "Lorenzo, do you remember when we went to the field where Chito slept?"

We were all outside watching the sunset from the casita, which had a high view of the whole city. From there, the "big picture" was not abstract. It was real, tangible, visible—we could just make out the Burger King sign towering beyond the border fence. The sun was blood red, and then the whole sky was washed with soft, liquid color. The city slowly retreated into the dark, and the lights, most of them naked bulbs dangling from ceilings and poles throughout the land-scape below, twinkled and burned in the blackening sky. "It is beauti-ful," I said to myself in astonishment, for it was the first time I had thought that all day. All the kids were standing near me, watching too. Boston said, "You can see everything from here. Everything."

THREE

Casas y Familias / Houses and Families

The next morning Maeve and I arrived at Mi Nueva Casa to find that no one had shown up for breakfast except shy David, who always smiled and rarely spoke. Among the boys, he was the only one to live with his mother in the neighborhood and so hung on the edge of Barrio Libre. But I knew where to find the others and headed up to Jesús' casita in Los Virreyes, hoping for another day roaming the city and filming.

Jesús must have heard my car scraping up the rocky hill; he catapulted out of the shack, a gaping smile on blue-smeared lips. The others, he told me, were within. The blue was paint, like a circle of misplaced lipstick—a residue from snorting up paint fumes from a Coke can or paper sack held up against the face like an oat bag. Boston staggered out behind him, equally drugged and evidently stunned by the blazing sun.

"*Bienvenido*, Lorenzo."

"I was hoping we could film today," I said in pointless frustration.

"*Sí,*" Boston shouted, his eyes spinning in his head. The others were beginning to tumble out of the shack, probably to see what the commotion was about.

David

"You film," Boston said, suddenly seized by an idea. He leaped atop a wobbly hillock of wood scraps and, holding up an imaginary microphone, bellowed, "Permit me to introduce you to the members of El Barrio Libre: Chito, Humberto, Ricardo, Jesús, y La Flor." Some of them went along with the act, but most ambled around in a distracted haze, vaguely embarrassed. The least drugged were Romel and Fanta—another couple—who lurked at the edge of the lot. He was checking the batteries in his flashlight, like any young husband about to go off to work. Romel would be leading a group of *pollos*—clandestine immigrants—through the tunnel and then robbing them of whatever scraps of money, belongings, or clothing they might have. One boy I did not know stared at me in blinking amazement, his face that of an Aztec sculpture.

Chito muttered to him that I was all right, but I suddenly realized that had I any sense, I should have been afraid. I was, after all, standing in the middle of what was generally considered a dangerous slum in the best of times, but I was alone with a video camera and about a dozen violent gang kids, every one of them stoned out of his mind.

But I was more disappointed than scared. Just as I was about to give up for the day, I noticed that Jesús was rubbing a swollen thumb. "Scorpion bite," he informed me calmly. "I have the prescription from the clinic, but I have no money to fill it."

"Let's go," I said. Jesús, suddenly less dizzy, climbed into the car, shouting good-natured insults out the window to his comrades as we rolled down the hill. I was grateful for a clear mission with a limited goal, and Jesús was happy for another car-borne adventure.

And no doubt hoping for more than medicine.

"Just give me the money—it should cost two hundred pesos—I'll go in for the prescription," he said as we pulled up to the *farmacia*, but I had learned at least that much by then and went in myself, with Jesús striding happily at my side. I paid the fifty pesos and threw in a papaya *paleta* from a street vendor outside. Jesús popped the ice in his mouth, smeared a dab of white cream on his scorpion bite, and strode cheerfully down the road toward town.

Later that day I sat at Mi Nueva Casa wondering what the hell we were doing. Boston's questions and the adventures filming in Nogales

VERO (LA FANTA)

began to look like an aberration—a brief respite from *"espray"* and the violent criminal life of the tunnel. I couldn't get that morning's drug scene out of my mind. Certainly I had known what they were up to, but seeing them all there like that was another matter. I suppose I was reacting, as people generally do, to inhalants, which occupy the bottom rung in our hierarchy of drugs. For the police, the Border Patrol, and the citizens of both sides of the border, nothing is lower than a glue or paint sniffer. People find the very idea revolting; perhaps they are disgusted and frightened by both the act and the sort of people who do it. The substances themselves seem the least "natural"—a fundamental violation of categories, a confusion that threatens our most basic sense of "what goes where." As for the sniffers themselves, they are the poorest of drug takers, for inhalants are the cheapest drug. Like the drunk who descends to turpentine, the sniffer or huffer of espray is by definition a kind of street slime. For all these reasons, there are no "programs" for them. Drunks may occasionally be inspired, and spirits may enter us through every kind of hallucinogenic plant and flower, but there is nothing of the sacred in espray. The kids themselves simply say, *"Me pone loco"*—"It makes me crazy."

I was shaken from my reveries by the bang of the iron door. Black silhouettes against the intense sunlight, they all strolled in—just in time for lunch. The house rules require attendance at morning classes. No lessons, no lunch. But the schooling was hardly more reliable than the kids. Teachers came and went rapidly, and the most recently hired had not shown up for more than a week. Besides, Ramona, angry and frustrated as she frequently was with them, could not stand to see the kids hungry, so she ushered them once again into the kitchen, and we watched them pile paper plates with steaming heaps of yellow and brown: spicy chorizo sausage, eggs, and beans. Jesús was sent around the corner with some pesos and returned with two huge plastic bottles of Pepsi and a hefty stack of hot corn tortillas. The kids hunched over the table, quieter than usual, rapidly spooning up the eggs and deftly rolling tortillas between their palms and popping them into their mouths, like logs into a fire.

"The espray makes them hungry," Ramona mumbled to me with resignation.

Suddenly Boston burst into laughter as Jorge, whacking the chili salsa bottle, sent a great shimmering scarlet glob spreading over his eggs. Now I understood the source of Jorge's nickname, "El Chamuco," the devil. I laughed despite myself, and the others looked up and smiled at my amusement. Guanatos, no doubt sensing my change of mood, leaned toward me with an irresistibly charming dimpled smile.

"Do you know Guadalajara, *mi tierra?*" he asked.

I said I did not, but Maeve, who had just joined us, said she had visited his hometown, and together they began to reminisce. Guanatos spoke with great pride of the city, as if he did not himself come from its farthest edge, an endless field of shacks spreading toward the horizon.

"There is the great market, San Juan de Dios—you know it—with goods from all of Mexico, and the most beautiful cathedral in all the country. In another church outside the city," he leaned toward us, away from the table at which the others continued to eat, "there is the Virgin of Zapopan—you must have heard of her, of all her miracles. The people come to her from everywhere; some come even on their knees. My aunt often goes there, and she took me once. I received a cure. Many lakes there are miraculous. The pilgrimage follows a road between hills for six or seven hours every night, until morning, until you arrive. Many do it [make the pilgrimage] on their knees. I know a woman who visited the Virgin with her son. He was beyond hope. She had promised to make the pilgrimage. And yes, . . . it is said that he was cured."

He turned suddenly toward me, holding me with his now serious eyes. "Do you believe in such things, Lorenzo? In miracles, in cures?" I blurted out awkwardly that I wasn't sure but that I thought there were many powerful things I did not know or understand. He took that as a yes, and leaning back, he smiled with satisfaction and continued his tour of the city.

"And there is of course the great square with mariachis. Guadalajara is the home of mariachi!"

We nodded with enthusiasm, saying that the city—everyone knew—was the most musical of Mexico. He agreed and, as if to prove the point, pushed his chair back from the table, hushed his comrades, and began to sing. Not a mariachi tune from his homeland, however. Guanatos's song was a ballad of this northern borderland, *un corrido*. He began uncertainly, in a broken, wavering whine, but soon found his mark. What had been thin became delicate, an impossibly sad ghost's voice singing from within a jail cell:

> On the tenth of May I was taken to prison, and in my cell I arrived.
> They gave me a letter that told me, "your mother has died."
> I called the jailer to ask permission to go back to see her.
> But he ignored me and would keep me in my pain unable to leave.
> I killed the jailer and that I don't repent
> Because I had to see my mother . . . and to her I went.

"Is it long since you've been in Guadalajara?" Maeve asked.

"Yes, and it is for that reason I want to go. I want to see my mother. But no, I think I can't go because of the rains. I was going to leave yesterday, but I couldn't; the train didn't go. There was a storm—even with hail—so everything was wet, and I didn't go. I want to go to see my mother; now I imagine how she is. I came here without asking her permission."

He looked down for a moment and then continued, "I have a lot of sisters; I am the only man in the house. I have a little sister, and another older than I am. We were left like dogs. It's that my father, well . . . never, never did you see someone like him. He is the reason I came here. If my parents had stayed together, none of this would have happened. If they had stayed together, we would have been taken care of from when we were young, and now that we are big, we could work, get around . . . but no. And now it is too late, for we are big, and that was when we were young. Isn't it true? Then, they could have continued to be my father and mother. But I want to go and see her if I can—my mother. Then I will return here and study hard."

He looked now as if he were picturing himself there.

"With my father the way he is, my aunts cannot see me, nor his mother, nor all his brothers—none of them can see me. When I wasn't a marijuana smoker, they called me one. They were already bitter against me. Well, then, because they didn't want me there, I left with my mother, and there the same thing happened. I haven't written; I don't really know my mother's address. I have always lived in the street. It's just that I want to go see my mother. Yes, like in that song I sang, I heard it in jail—I was there myself—on the tenth of May."

Guanatos looked up at Maeve and me, adding the final note that perhaps he thought would work best.

"I would like not to use drugs. I would like to calm down. Yes, I would like to stop. But when I am here, all the temptations start. It is very difficult with my friends—all of them always drugging themselves. If I took the train, it costs like 210 pesos to get there."

"We can help you get down there, if you like," I offered without thinking, "but what about school?"

"I will go next week and return for school by September," he said beaming with excitement. "The teacher doesn't come now, and a new one will take some weeks to find. By then I'll be back!"

I wondered aloud whether his fellow Guadalajaran, El Boston, might want to join him on the trip. Guanatos jumped up and went out to the courtyard, where his friend was carefully wiping every speck of grime from a pair of glowing white sneakers. As it turned out, Boston was unable or unwilling to make the journey at the time, and Guanatos would take the thousand-mile train trip on his own.

When we were alone, Maeve asked me whether I had done the right thing in offering to help Guanatos return to Guadalajara. Of course, I didn't know, and the more I thought about it, the less certain I was, about that and everything else. I looked at the after-lunch scene, a scattering of sated, sleepy *cholos* slumped on seam-bursting vinyl sofas in the increasingly humid, dead heat of late August. They were all mesmerized by an incredibly noisy and violent kung fu film—their favorite fare. What, indeed, were we doing? Nothing we did, nothing that anyone did, seemed to have the intended result. Were we simply providing a feeding station, keeping them healthy and rested enough to continue terrorizing the innocent in the tunnel that ran nearly under the very room in which we all sat? Was there any chance that in giving them something like a home to come to—however limited— we were seducing them into better or at least safer world? Or was this "home" at best a sadistic tease, a fleeting and partial view of something they could not keep, that abruptly ended for them? The sign on the door of Mi Nueva Casa reads, "No one over eighteen permitted"—a stipulation of the juvenile delinquency prevention money that funds the operation. The kids' lives were bad enough now, but would become dramatically worse when that age line was crossed. Once they were eighteen, banned from Mi Nueva Casa or not, when next arrested on either side of the border, they would be adults facing the drug gang–run federal prisons of the United States or the stinking black holes of Mexico.

At that moment, Flor's baby, Davidcito, burst into a gurgling, spitting laugh. She was bouncing him on her lap as Jesús tickled and poked his sides. El Boston swaggered by and deftly swung the delighted infant into the air, and everyone's eyes—smiling as if there were no better place or moment to be—watched their own Davidcito. They were not a perfect family, but they were a family. In a moment, they were all standing at the door like a troop of nomads, and I offered to run them and their belongings up the several miles of blazing hot city streets to Jesús' casita.

So once again we were together, belting out tunes with the radio, rocketing around Nogales. As we approached the Stupid Dummy statue, Chito casually noted that Flor's father lived just up the road. I had heard no mention of this fact from anybody and wondered whether the adults running the Casa even knew that Flor—who with her baby was at the center of everybody's thoughts and worries—had family so close by. I looked at her in the rearview mirror.

"We can go there, if you like," she said with little apparent interest. We turned off the main road and found our way to the dead end of a deeply rutted mud road on the edge of a vast and notorious *colonia*, Los Tapiros.

Guanatos and Boston said goodbye and went off to check the windshield-washing action at the Dummy.

"Up there," Jesús motioned, and we all fell in line behind him, picking our way up a steep sand-and-rock slope to the first houses, each one clinging to the dirt with logs and sticks that looked as if they would give way before the first serious rains. The third house up was Flor's, a tidy pink cottage cantilevered at a perilous angle out of

the hillside. Outside the screen door was a tiny but carefully manicured garden, in its midst a small tree that succeeded against all odds
in offering shade in the broiling afternoon. Under it, Jesús and Chito
took shelter while Flor and I went to the frail screen door.

A man, evidently risen from sleep, answered. He stood there blinking under a soft vaquero's hat—his skin somehow pallid beneath a la-
borer's tan, his long frame bent like a question mark as his soft eyes
took in his daughter and this unlikely stranger. "Come in," he mur-
mured, mildly confused by the visit. As soon as his eyes focused on
the baby, however, he seemed to come alive, and in another moment
he was wide awake and babbling nonsense into Davidcito's chortling
face. He turned again to me, and I explained that I was working with
Flor and her friends at Mi Nueva Casa. He nodded and then looked to
his daughter. But she was already doing what she was supposed to,
taking a pitcher of lemonade from the refrigerator and pouring tall
glasses for us.

"Sit, sit," Flor's father invited me and called into the back room,
from which a young woman came a moment later. "I am Myrna, Flor's
sister," she told me, a fact I would never have guessed from her appearance. She, too, was pretty, but with skin many shades lighter and
with a shorter and frosted hairdo that made her seem far more grown
up than her twenty-three years.

"Ay, papito," she said, taking her little nephew from her father
and standing him up on the table before her. Flor continued to busy
herself like a proud little housewife, setting the glasses—each with a
sliver of lemon—before us. She sat down finally, indicating with a
small flourish that we were to enjoy our drinks.

So we did, and I happily sipped the cool, delicious liquid as Myrna
chatted away about a wedding that the family had recently been to
in the desert town of Caborca, from which they had come to Nogales
when Flor was only a baby.

"It was a great occasion," Myrna told us, "with many guests and
wonderful food. We each received one of these," and she pointed behind her where a shimmering white plastic memento of flowers and
photos was newly nailed to the wall.

My eyes began then to take in the other decorations, the home that Flor's old family—as opposed to her new one in the shack—had struggled to make here in two small but neat rooms teetering on the edge of the colonia. The plywood walls had been painted and papered in soft pastels, and a dark wood hutch was nearly full of plates and trinkets. Christ and His Holy Mother looked down from the wall behind the table, just next to the wedding memento, and a number of little family snapshots were tacked here and there around the place. The wiring was roughly stapled to the walls, but there was electricity, and the low hum of the old fridge in the corner sounded luxurious.

"I work at one of the *maquiladoras*," Myrna told me. "The work is not difficult, but it is very boring, and we get only forty-two pesos each day. You know what that is now in dollars? That's right, maybe five, maybe six. Whatever it is today, tomorrow it will be less. So you see how it is with us. Papá works on the building sites when he can, I at the maquiladora, and my little brother in a hotel. Together we make enough only for this."

Her father handed Flor a twenty-peso note, and she turned to me, asking if I would like to accompany her to the shop. We stepped out into the blinding afternoon, and our friends, whom I had absolutely forgotten had been waiting under the tree, popped up, ready for the next venture. We headed on foot into the colonia, passing through a world filled with families cooking lunch, families washing cars, families greeting other families.

"Hola!" The voice came from above us, where I turned to see a squat, shirtless man on the edge of a tiny yard that sloped down from a little brick home to a crumbling earthen edge a yard or two above the path we were taking.

"Who is your friend?" he asked, sweat dripping from a thick black mustache that made it difficult to judge whether he was being friendly or not. Flor smiled up at him, and I introduced myself and asked if he was working there in the yard.

"Come up and see! I am working here on the future of my family!"

We took the path around and found Eduardo—another Guadalajaran as it turned out—standing, rag in hand, beside a very worn *taquería,* a rolling metal taco stand.

"I bought this for very little because it needs so very much!" he said. "But if I can get it finished and into the streets before too long, I hope to see money coming in instead of going out." He laughed at himself and whistled sharply at a swirling group of dogs and children chasing each other on the road beneath us. They were all his, he told us, and both dogs—large spotted creatures well suited for life in the colonia—were named Paco.

"The same name?" I asked, "How do you tell them apart, or how do they know which of them you are calling?"

"Does it matter?" he asked. "Do you know Guadalajara?" The second time I had been asked that in one day.

"Only the song," I answered, and without a pause he began to sing it. One of my favorite mariachi tunes, it's a punchy, multiharmonic tribute to the grandeur of the city that he, like Boston and Guanatos, had left for one of the ugliest places on God's Earth. Jesús, who had been standing around waiting patiently but without much interest, now listened intently. We all laughed, clapped at the end, and made our way on to the shop—another house really, but with a room full of groceries for sale—and then back along another path that hugged the edge of the hill to Flor's father's house. From this height, I could see the entire colonia—hill after rolling hill of brick, stick, or cardboard homes. I walked behind Jesús and Flor, who held hands like the most romantic of child lovers.

When we had taken our leave from Flor's family, I renewed my offer to drive everyone back to the casita in Los Virreyes. We stopped at a huge flea market so that Chito and Jesús could search out the latest cassettes. I was staring out the car window at the bustling scene when Flor, who had remained in the car with me, suddenly spoke.

"Look, Lorenzo, these are the photos of my *quinceañera.*"

In her lap, she was holding a bulky white-plastic photo album that she had taken from her father's house. In it were perhaps a dozen dim snapshots taken at her fifteenth birthday party not quite a year earlier. I had heard about the party, which had been given not by her family but by Mi Nueva Casa. One of the volunteers there had searched long and hard for a dress that would look good on Flor's still delicate but several-months pregnant body. Another had found the gift Flor most wanted: a "Selena Barbie"—a Latina version of that iconic doll, nearly a relic of the murdered Tejana star.

"This is Ricardo," she said, pointing to a murky photo of a slim boy only slighter older than herself, "the father of Davidcito." She turned up to me with a face as sentimental, as ultimately inscrutable, as that of any adolescent girl—which she now had become. Was she still mooning over her last boyfriend, the father of her baby, or was she simply in love with the event of her party, as any Mexican girl is brought up to be? How, I wondered—this time aloud—could she prefer the world of the dirt-floored shack, espray, and the tunnel to what seemed wonderful in comparison, the calm and even pretty little home that her own family was struggling so to make at the edge of Colonia Los Tapiros?

"It's that . . . I guess I never really got along with them, with my father, sister, and brother. They're always saying things to me, telling me that I am bad. It's that they don't take drugs, so they don't approve of me." She smiled wanly. At that point, Chito and Jesús returned, happily diving into the car. Chito joined me in the front and popped in a cassette with a border rap song on the joys of escaping the law, and we rolled again, taking Chito and the little family to Los Virreyes.

FOUR

Tomando fotos / Taking Photos

We were heading north along Obregón toward El Viachi, the massive Nogales supermarket with a huge pig's head sculpture made of chorizo, when we spotted the kids. "Look over there," said Mi Nueva Casa volunteer shopper Claudia, tapping a long red manicured nail on the window. It was Flor, Jesús, Juanito, Jorge, and—bouncing on Jorge's shoulders—little Davidcito. They had evidently come from Jesús' shack in Los Virreyes and were making their determined way along the main drag of the city. Whatever they had done the night before, they had risen early, and now with a bit less than a mile to go, they would arrive in time for breakfast and school lessons.

And so it went at Mi Nueva Casa. Days of determined effort followed by days "missing in action." More and more often I sought the kids in the other places I knew they frequented—the shack in Los Virreyes, of course, but also the Stupid Dummy windshield-washing station, and the tiny municipal park beyond it. In the way of their world—where things change suddenly and yet somehow never change at all—those days in the streets had made me, if not a friend, at least an apparently trusted and even welcomed part of

juanito

their daily lives. Whether we were roaming the city, relaxing at Mi Nueva Casa, or cooling off in the municipal pool, we had grown used to and fond of each other.

The pool, in fact, had proven a particularly comfortable space, an almost neutral zone where, dressed in donated bathing suits and able to jump, dunk, and loll, the kids were free from the constraints of both Mi Nueva Casa and their own Barrio Libre rules of comportment. Couples, even Jesús and Flor, separated for the afternoon. The two or three girls who came would usually bob around the pool on a rented inner tube—chatting heads together inside the circle, languorously kicking legs pointed out. When they tired of that, Flor or La Fanta would ask me for a swimming lesson.

Pausing between attempts at the crawl, Fanta seemed to drop her aggressive front and even laughed at herself. She spoke a little of her frustrations with Romel. Although I saw her nearly every day, I knew little of her life, other than that she was Romel's girlfriend and that they did not seem to get on all that well. If Romel was lazy and moody, Fanta was aggressive and explosive. Now, however, she seemed relaxed, so I asked her about her life.

"I came to Nogales when I was four, with my mother, stepfather, and one brother. Since then, I have younger sisters, too. I quit school when I was ten. I don't know. I just didn't like school. I live with my family still, when I am not in the tunnel." She smiled slyly.

I asked her to tell me more about the tunnel.

"I go in alone or with my cousin, Negro," she continued in a lively whisper. "My mother tells me that I must not go into the tunnel because it is a dangerous and evil place, but I am disobedient and don't care about the consequences—death." She was a little dramatic but still whispering.

"How," I asked her, "do people die?"

"They die from bullets, knives, beatings, and from drugs." She paused for a moment and then continued, reminiscing. "I went the first time with a guy who told me not to be afraid. But I didn't know him well, so I was more afraid than I would have been alone! I remember we went in with a flashlight, and everything was very dark."

"I go often now. Sometimes I have my daughter with me,

sometimes my mother looks after her," she paused to look over at wild little Sayra, who was playing under a tree. "At fourteen I was pregnant, and at fifteen I had my child. She is one and a half now."

I asked her if Romel was the father.

"No," she replied. "That was Salvador. We were together for a while. We had sex the first time in a train car. We were half-crazy on spray, and the second time we were together was at a friend's house. Then I was pregnant. But he married another woman and left the barrio. I think he didn't marry me because my stepfather didn't want him around."

I asked her how much money they could get in the tunnel; I had heard wild numbers.

"Maybe two to five hundred pesos. It depends on how long we are there and the luck, of course. Sometimes we are there for a few days at a time, sometimes two or three hours, sometimes one night."

It was difficult to imagine spending so much time in those damp, dark, stinking passages. "How do you pass the time there, waiting for people to come?" I asked.

"Most of the time I make myself crazy with a can of paint that lasts say from three in the afternoon to seven at night. You do it in a soda can—spray it in and then take it through your mouth. You do like one whole can of paint if you want it to last a long time. Sometimes I don't want it to last, so I do less."

I was still trying to get a sense of just how much and how many drugs they used, so I asked her.

"I do the paint almost every day. I don't much like marijuana. And beer I almost never drink. Once in a while I take coca. But it isn't like I am addicted. If I want, I can leave it. It isn't like I can't live without it; whenever I would want to, I could give it up." She paused and, frowning, added, "Before Sayra, I had another baby who was born dead. The doctor said that he couldn't develop well because of my use of drugs."

Fanta wanted to return to the topic of life in the tunnel, and, smiling again, she whispered to me, "Once I took down [robbed] some people by myself. I was a little high, and I heard footsteps. When I jumped up to see who it was, I saw that it was a guy. He was crazy on paint. Then I saw some women there, and I told them to put up their hands to the ceiling. I got three hundred pesos from each woman." She was proud and happy to remember and recount the incident. I simply nodded and returned to the business of swimming instruction.

A few of the boys took lessons with me as well, though most were too impatient and perhaps too proud for instruction. They would head for the high board, six meters up, and hurl themselves through the air, cannonballing into the pool with as much splashed water and fanfare as possible. The smaller they were, the more emphatic the gesture. Tiny Oscar, a born comedian who was thirteen but still shorter than five feet tall, would announce his upcoming Olympic dives—"This one gets silver!"—and then throw himself spinning off the board, howling all the way down. The older boys swam as much as they could manage or tossed a ball around in the water. Resting under the shade of a poolside cottonwood, we would suck on *paletas* and chat about all our favorite foods. The smaller boys played like monkeys, poking at the older kids until they were finally sent sprawling by a karate kick. Little Toñito was particularly fond of pestering Guanatos that way, but when he tired of wrestling, he would inevitably end up draped affectionately over his older pal's shoulder.

Often enough, one or another of the boys would paddle up beside me in the pool and, as we leaned together at the side, tell me the more intimate details of his life. Fanta's boyfriend, Romel, was difficult and aggressive with an audience, but clearly among the smartest of the kids, and when a private moment was possible, he would reveal something of himself. I had noticed that he would occasionally use an English phrase with me, and one day I asked him about it. He answered, at first in English,

"I lived in Chicago and the state of Washington with my father. He worked on a ranch there—and was also a drug dealer."

He continued in Spanish.

"I was born in Guadalajara, Jalisco. In 1983, I was three, and they put my father in jail. My brother was one, and the youngest, two months. At that time, my father was a cop. He used to get coke for my mother, but he was a big womanizer.

Toñito

"One day, he was in a cantina, drunk, when he saw a man kissing my mother. He killed him. They gave him only five years; because he had been a policeman, they didn't give him more. He told my mother that if he found her when he got out, he would kill her. She fled. She changed her name and left us.

"In 1989, I went to Chicago with my father. He was busy, and I was alone a lot and didn't know anybody in Chicago. I spent many days sleeping in the street, and some *cholos* there picked me up. We spoke Spanish, and I told them I didn't know anybody. They took me to their house, then they took me to the store and bought me clothes and fed me. They were going to put me in school, but it was vacation time."

I nodded and was thinking he was lucky to find such friendly compatriots in distant Chicago when he continued, "We did about seven robberies together. We stole shotguns, swords, and knives. The police never caught us. We sold the weapons. We used the shotgun and little pistols. They killed one guy, but I never killed anyone.

"Then the police arrested me, in the street. They took photos of me, but they couldn't prove that I took part in any robbery. They took me in a plane to jail in another city. I spent eight months there. When I got out, I couldn't find my father at first. When I did, he took me to Washington State. But we had to leave there because my father was in trouble over taxes, so they sent us away to Nogales. My papá and I are prohibited from returning to Washington."

"How is it in Nogales for you?" I asked.

"I don't like Nogales much because of the police here. I live in Fanta's house. For money, I rob the people that pass in the tunnel."

"Does that get you much money?"

"Depending on luck, I can get two or three hundred dollars, and I use it to amuse myself with drugs."

"Which drugs?" I asked, thinking of Boston's questions and my conversation with Fanta.

"I smoke marijuana. Coca less, but you can get some for twenty or thirty pesos. I also take spray. Yesterday I did coca through the nose, and I gave myself a head! I have injected *chiva* [heroin] and coca only one time."

ROMEL

Then he appeared to change the subject, saying, "I am going to see my father again soon. He has been father and mother to us; he has taken much care of us, and now he is sixty-five years old."

But just when I thought the conversation had taken a sentimental turn again, Romel added, "He gets drugs in Jalisco, and it's easy enough for us to pass them over to the other side. I speak English, more or less, so that my brothers and I can deliver the drugs to the other side. We divide the drugs into different packets and take them to the customers. My little brother waits outside and watches. We are armed to protect ourselves. One time some blacks wanted to rob us."

Throughout our conversation, Romel's tone was flat, neither bragging nor complaining—simply reporting. But another time at the pool, he turned to me in the middle of a game of keep-away. "Do you see that guy over there, on the far side of the pool? He is my brother. He lives in Colonia Buenos Aires. We haven't spoken for several years." This time, his eyes were filled with hurt and fury.

Boston, too, would take the opportunity to speak more of his past. He talked more of his life in Guadalajara, where he had shared a three-room house with a mother, father, and brother.

"When my mother was alive, my father took good care of all of us, but she was killed in a car accident, and when she was gone, he no longer paid attention. Whenever I went to him with a problem, he gave me an excuse—he always had to go off to some important meeting with somebody. He took drugs, too. So did his brother, my uncle, and my own brother—coca and marijuana."

Thinking of his interview questions, I asked Boston about school. Clearly he had been there long enough to learn how to read and write, which was not the case with his pal Jesús, for example.

"I went to school for many years, but it always bored me. Home bored me, too, so at nine I left school and home and became a *niño vato*—a street kid. I didn't know what to do, and I wandered out to see places I didn't know. I didn't care what happened, and I lost my respect for elders and everything. By the time I was ten years old, I would go around selling pills and getting into fights. A friend of mine then was stabbed in the heart and died, but everyone was taking pills and marijuana—all my friends in the street. I started with pills and marijuana at ten, cocaine at twelve, morphine at thirteen, peyote at fourteen, crack and heroin at fifteen."

Even though I knew that he and the others did a variety of drugs, the length of the list stunned me, as did the bland manner in which he reported it. I asked him whether he was taking all those drugs now.

"Morphine, tobacco, cocaine, marijuana," he recited calmly. "When I take drugs, it makes me hungry and makes me think a lot, but it doesn't make me *cabrón* [aggressively manly]."

"And the money for all that?" I asked, already knowing the answer.

"I go into the tunnel now. I used to rob places with a friend of mine—another *morro* [guy] from Guadalajara. He was twenty. You remember when I took you to the train station? Well, the guy I met there—I told you about him—he and I used to rob people down there. We would get clothes and have a bath at a construction site nearby, change, and leave around 5:30 or 6:00 in the afternoon. Or we would break into houses. Once we found two packets of dollars—four thousand bucks! That was the most we ever got. Later on, he left for Tucson and never came back. Since then, I get money mainly in the tunnel—two or three hundred pesos maybe."

I asked him how he spent his time in the tunnel.

"We'll be there and wait for hours, then a group will come. Sometimes six or seven groups like that will pass in one day. Sometimes I will be in there a long time, sleeping, taking drugs, passing the hours of my life in the tunnel."

One afternoon we were all standing outside the pool, waiting for a bus. I asked Boston, Guanatos, and Chito where they would be spending the evening. *"P' allá"* [por allá], Boston replied, looking north. Over there. He meant the United States. When speaking "locally," they never said the words "United States" or "Mexico." It was simply *"p' acá"* or *"p' allá."* Over here or over there. Or else, *"el otro lado."* The other side. The two sides were separated by *la línea.* A strangely familiar way of talking about this most emphatic of borders, but appropriate given their lives and the lives of most people living on the Mexican side. For these kids especially, the border was both friend and enemy—but in both cases, intimate. The fact of it created a two-part world—two sets of resources to exploit, two sets of dangers to avoid, and the kids took self-conscious pride in their ability to move easily, casually, and effectively through their bilateral world.

"Where did you buy that?"

"Over there."

"Where were you yesterday evening, over here or over there?"

"Over here."

And so on.

"I am going to Tucson," Boston continued, "I've got a job there in a restaurant."

"Me too," said Chiguile, who had drifted up beside us. He was the dark boyfriend of La Halloween—so named for her fondness for makeup. She also had a tattoo across her belly, which was beginning to stretch as she swelled with child. Chiguile, too, was unusually decorated; his tattoos had shimmered under the surface of the water. All the kids sported at least a triangle of three dots on the wrist: "mi vida loca," Flor had explained, my crazy life. But Chiguile's arms and chest carried more personal messages, including the name of the girlfriend who had preceded La Halloween. I remembered seeing their names paired in graffiti inside the tunnel.

"How will you go to Tucson?" I asked.

"Easy," Boston replied. "We will go through the tunnel and then hop a freight train." Chiguile nodded.

They spoke as if the journey were the most casual of passages rather than one that brought them through several miles of stinking, death-ridden tunnel and an elicit sixty-mile ride between the jolting cars of a freight train—a ride that several had listed in Boston's interview as sometimes bringing them near death. In fact, a year earlier, death had come for one kid. He had missed in his attempt to swing up between the moving freight cars, and his body had been cut in two by the scissoring metal.

Over the course of the summer, I was filling out the answers to many of Boston's questions. I knew the kids' names, their nicknames, and where they were from. In a few cases, I had been to the homes of those families who lived in Nogales. Of the twenty odd kids I had

La Halloween

met, only five were girls, and they all had family in Nogales—though
their relations with them, as with Flor, varied from friendly to hostile. The boys were far more likely to have come to Nogales alone or at
least without adults: Boston and Guanatos from as far away as Guadalajara, most of the others from somewhere in the state of Sonora. But
Boston's questions had mostly dwelt on the life of the barrio, and of
that, too, I was beginning to both see and hear more every day.

Even Flor—who, until our trip to her home, had said almost
nothing—seemed far less guarded. She had risked revealing something to me of her family difficulties, and I had neither scolded nor
ignored her, so she could tell me more, sometimes only with her eyes,
about her fears and desires. She often talked of Davidcito. He was, in
fact, her second baby; the first—born to her at the age of thirteen—
had not lived more than a couple of months when his lungs failed apparently because of birth defects from a drugged pregnancy. With
Davidcito, she did not appear to be so bad a mother as you might
imagine, at least in the setting of Mi Nueva Casa. Mostly she attended
to her baby's needs—giving him her breast at frequent intervals,
playing with him, and bathing him in a plastic basin at the feet of
Doñas Ramona and Loida. If she were not holding him, someone else,
usually Jesús or Boston, was. I saw her being careless with him only
once, nearly tossing him onto the sofa so that her hands were free
to attack another girl who had threatened her. But we all knew that
Davidcito was spending his nights in the casita, in a dirt-floored
shack, with scorpions on the ground, its air choked with paint fumes.
Though he seemed miraculously healthy and happy, we wondered
whether he would not be better off somewhere—anywhere—else. It
was easy to forget all these problems, though, as we watched Flor,
sweet and caring, busy packing up the bales of pampers and a sack
of baby clothes that one of the American volunteers had smuggled
across the border.

In an instinctive and affectionate way, Flor also grew closer to
Maeve, who was busy with her camera at Mi Nueva Casa. She was trying to find a way to teach the kids something of value and decided to
hold a regular "class" every Wednesday afternoon. The class rarely
went smoothly and never lasted very long, but once there, the kids

that came showed great enthusiasm for the enterprise. Maeve succeeded in teaching Flor and a few of the other kids how to operate everything from a Polaroid to a fully manual vintage Pentax, once again belying what we had been told about their abilities and attention span. Maeve was also trying to help make Mi Nueva Casa more like a home by covering its walls with a series of portraits of the kids. Flor and Chito decided they would help her. They took their own photos and acted as her assistants, handling equipment, directing subjects, discussing the virtues of black and white over color. "Next victim," Chito would shout into the house and then bring another kid out into the sun-drenched courtyard. "You must stand here," he told each one. "That's where we all stand." And so they would. Each one would strike his or her own pose, some looking like they always did, but others becoming suddenly "other"—posing, pretending, revealing—proud, hopeful, frightened, distant.

The kids, especially Chito and Flor, became increasingly conscious of the usefulness of the camera to record and validate the moments of their lives, which was hardly a foreign notion in Mexico, where every public occasion finds street photographers memorializing the event for those who can afford it. But now they had cameras readily available, and they themselves were able to use them whenever and wherever the occasion demanded, as when we were all together on the day of Guanatos's departure for Guadalajara. We waited with him that morning in the cavernous, sweltering bunker of a station, along with families still stretched out on blankets from the night before. Guanatos held his ticket tightly in one hand and a plastic shopping bag Ramona had packed with clothes and snacks in the other. We were at a loss as to what to do with the remaining moments when Flor, like a compulsive aunt at a wedding, began to arrange us for photos. She had to have every possible shot of Guanatos, passing Davidcito around like a prop and making one after the other of us join or leave the photo.

Back at Mi Nueva Casa, life alternated between the heat-stilled calm of most days and the occasional event—an arrest, perhaps a visit from a life-weary mother or, more rarely, father looking for or checking up on the progress of her wayward child, or sometimes the arrival of new kids. Usually these newcomers showed up by themselves or in pairs—often brothers (like Noe and Chuy and their neighbor Diego). Once, an entire family—a mother and three children—appeared at the door and was invited in for a meal. They had come up to the border from the far south, Michoacán, and spoke with the soft accents of their homeland. The mother had come north looking for work, but said that she was not considering crossing the border. Even though she had found employment at a maquiladora, there was no place for her and her family to live, and the salary was not adequate to keep them anywhere but the street. The oldest daughter was pregnant and looked hopeless, and an eleven-year-old son had never heard of New York, but the middle child, a girl of fourteen, was clear-eyed, sharp, and bizarrely optimistic considering their circumstances. She told us that she had been reading and had decided to become a computer scientist. They ate with us for several days and then stopped coming. We never saw them again. I could not help wondering what had happened to them. Did they decide to cross the border into the United States? If they went through the tunnel, had the kids let them pass through without robbing them?

One morning late in the summer, two new kids showed up. They were both smiling. One, named Marco Antonio, was a delicate, stunningly handsome boy of about fourteen. His companion, Juán Manuel, was twelve, but seemed much younger—a dancing puppet of a kid, half covered in burn-scarred flesh. They had just eaten breakfast and were only delighted to work it off cleaning up Mi Nueva Casa. Little Juán Manuel danced the old mop around the kitchen floor, twirling and pressing the frayed rope strands into the form of a sopping octopus, delighting himself and us with the game. Marco Antonio was more seriously pushing a rag along every surface he could find.

Loida filled us in. The two boys had been waiting at the door when they opened that morning. They had spent several nights on the street, during which time they had found each other and heard—so they told her—that they could find a meal at Mi Nueva Casa. They were hoping for that and more. A way in. A way out.

"The little one, Juán Manuel, is from Colima—in the south," Loida explained. "The other is from Santa Ana."

That town we knew well. Just sixty-five miles down the road, it

MOE

was like all desert villages, either under a cloud of dust or streaming with water. Marco had a family there, which he had left for no one knew what reason. But it was difficult to imagine how his friend—a scruffy waif without a centavo—had managed to get himself from Colima up to this border outpost, more than fifteen hundred miles. All we knew is that he had come alone. "The burns," Loida said, "are from when he was very young."

Juán Manuel followed me into the schoolroom where we perused a wall map together, locating his home and tracing his journey. He seemed bright and impossibly buoyant. The worst part of the trip had been the previous nights in Nogales, when some evil bastard had followed them through the night streets, leaving them no moment of peace. It was the only part of his story he did not smile in the telling.

Hoping to help them feel at home, Maeve offered to take their photos to add to the portrait gallery by then growing on the walls, which the two boys had been eyeing. They seemed very pleased at the notion, but Boston, who was sauntering through the kitchen at the moment, muttered to her, "You don't have to take their photos; they are not of Barrio Libre." For the adults of Mi Nueva Casa, the photos were meant both to record and to help create a family, but for the kids that family was Barrio Libre and did not include every waif who blew in off the street.

The two boys stood waiting. I wasn't sure if they had heard Boston. Juán Manuel was still beaming, but Marco Antonio stared ahead with visible uncertainty.

Among his questions, Boston had asked, "Have you always dressed as a cholo?" Marco Antonio and Juán Manuel had not yet begun. Their hair was too long and not combed correctly. Beneath the street grime, Juán Manuel was looking, as much as he could manage, like his mother would have wanted. He smoothed his buttoned-down, brightly patterned shirt. At least it wasn't tucked in, but his straight-legged pants met his shoes at the ankles. Marco was incredibly filthy. His pants were also too narrow and short, but the great sack of a striped T-shirt had possibilities, if the wide blotch and streaks of alley dirt could be removed.

Boston, I think, saw them not only as outside the barrio, but as

CHUY

not even cholos—the wider category of street culture that must be performed in speech, clothing, and general manner. As if to show them how, Boston strode by with loping cholo disdain, oversize T-shirt billowing over wide, baggy, black jeans, and, of course, gleaming white tennies. He sank laconically into the sofa.

Little Juán Manuel followed Maeve out for his photo, beaming as if he were off to a ride at the circus. Marco followed as well, but seemed far less certain of the event. He looked into and through the camera lens, with unsettlingly deep yet tentative eyes.

I went into the living room to be with Boston and the others, taking a moment to survey their clothes. Beneath the individual variations, they were, in fact, all in uniform. Those who had on sleeveless white T-shirts tucked them into their belted pants. Others wore oversize short-sleeved or sports-team T-shirts favoring such slogans as *La Raza* outside low-waisted, baggy pants, preferably jeans. The girls were similarly dressed, but did not wear the make-up fashionable among their Chicana counterparts in the United States—except for La Halloween, that is.

In this attention to dress, of course, they were like all adolescents I had ever met. I remembered the high schools I had myself attended or later observed, where the student population was divided into three or four "tribes" always distinguished by crucial elements of dress and speech. The names changed over the years—hoods, greasers, collegians, preppies, surfers, heavy metal freaks, skaters, hippies, heads—but the essential structural requisites remained the same. Walk the walk, talk the talk, dress right, and listen to the right music. Within any of these tribes, there were clans: the small bands of friends that shared more specific and exclusive elements of culture as well as a private history.

The street kids here were no different. Juán Manuel and Marco Antonio had arrived, the new kids on the block, and had to be shown the line that separated them from the tribe and the clan. It was an opportunity for Boston and his friends to perform their identity, but it was also a chance for instruction: this is how to dress and behave, they were saying; learn it, and you have passed over the first hurdle in becoming one of us. Of course, the demonstrated distance and disdain made the lone outsider want to belong.

Juán Manuel

To join the cholo tribe and Barrio Libre clan, they would have to learn to perform the culture in dress, talk, and general behavior. However, it struck me that music was an interesting exception to the usual narrowness of the adolescent search for identity. The kids certainly liked the latest street rap, but they were always happy to hear almost any kind of Mexican music and would sing along with anything from mariachi tunes to the border ballads, whether traditional or contemporary stories of the triumphs of *narcotraficantes*.

So perhaps the clothes, simple though they were, were a particular focus. Whenever clothes were donated to Mi Nueva Casa, they were selected not only by size, but also according to condition and appropriateness. Luckily, lots of baggy T-shirts came in. The oversize pants were more rare, and the sneakers—tennies—with the right look and name were the rarest and most valuable commodity. They were a crucial element of cholo costume and performance, made by Indonesian women for seventy-five cents an hour, then marketed all over the world by millions of dollars of advertisement as the single most important way to personal fulfillment and worldly success. Their value was assured by the price paid for them in the shop or, more brutally, on the street. We call it globalization. Even if Boston and his friends were unaware of the full extent of the life of that commodity and of the others they used to create their lives, they certainly operated in their own local internationalism.

"Where did you get the tennies?" I asked Boston.

"P' allá"—"Over there," he replied.

Later that afternoon, as Maeve and I were walking back from Mi Nueva Casa to the border gate, Marco Antonio and Juán Manuel followed us out, perhaps hoping that they could cross with us, but also interested in finding out more about this border world. "The tunnel," Marco Antonio asked us, "is it dangerous?"

We told him that it was dangerous, that many bad people were there and many others were hurt or killed.

"Yes," said Marco Antonio, nodding his head in agreement, "but many pass through here *por el otro lado* [to the other side]."

"Is that the tunnel?" Juán Manuel asked, gesturing toward a small niche in a wall on the side of a building. His eyes were filled with

Marco Antonio

wonder and excitement. Maeve said that it was not and cautioned them again about the dangers of the tunnel.

How, I thought, are they going to survive here? We gave them enough money to buy some food, but not so much as to be dangerous to carry, and bid them a reluctant good-bye. The hardy band of Barrio Libre, I realized, was only a fraction of the kids passing through this place. Some would get to the other side of the fence into the United States, but most would vanish into the streets or return to whence they came. In between, a few of them would find Mi Nueva Casa, where they would get some meals and typically a cool reception from the Barrio kids, who mostly carried on as if the newcomers were not there. That was the flip side of the clan identity, of course: their closeness depended on drawing a firm line between themselves and others—outsiders. Exclusion would make most newcomers want to join, to be a part. So I suppose I should not have been surprised when, only a week later, I ran into Marco Antonio on the street. I had not recognized the cholo who approached me, I thought to ask me for money. His head was nearly shorn, and he sported a great, baggy T-shirt over jeans. And tennies.

"How are you, Lorenzo?" he asked smiling broadly. He was, he told me, washing cars on the streets—a job, I knew, that frequently meant collusion with car break-in experts and an apprenticeship for more lucrative and dangerous jobs, including some in the tunnel. As for Juán Manuel, Marco Antonio had not seen him in days and had heard that he had returned to Colima.

Not long afterward, Maeve and I were standing over the tunnel entrance just down the street from Mi Nueva Casa. Maeve was trying to find a way of photographing it that would convey some sense of what it meant to the kids.

"Do you take pictures of the tunnel?" a woman's voice asked.

We looked up to see a woman somewhere in her thirties, accompanied by a small man who kept several feet behind her. She wore tight black jeans, a sleeveless black top, and a gold-chained handbag over her shoulder. She might have been out on a date, but the hot breeze blew loose, long black hair away from a face weary and streaked with tears. Her large brown eyes were desperately sad.

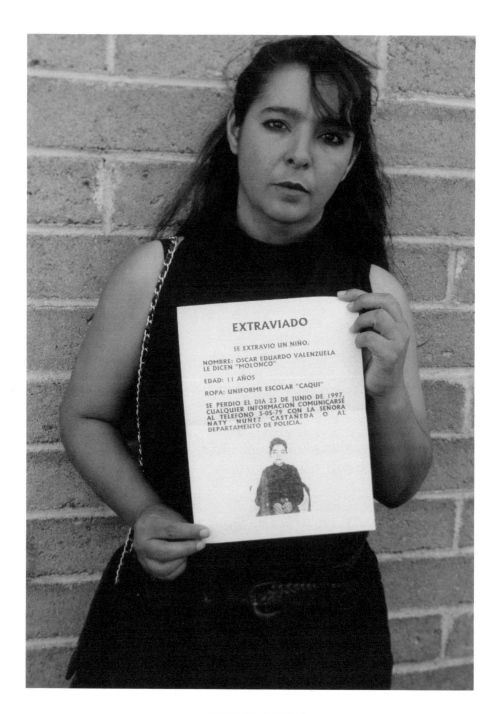

EXTRAVIADO (LOST)

"Have you seen him?" she asked us, showing us a sheet of paper with a photocopied portrait of a young boy. Beneath it was the large word, *EXTRAVIADO*—LOST. The text explained that eleven-year-old Roberto, also known as Molonco, had been last seen in his khaki school uniform some days before.

"My brother and I have looked everywhere," she told us. He nodded seriously. "But we cannot find him. I ask all the street kids I meet and show them this photo, but they claim to know nothing. Nobody knows anything. Are you reporters? Can you take my picture with the poster so that maybe someone will see who knows where my son is?"

We explained that we were not journalists, but were working at Mi Nueva Casa and were also doing a book on the tunnel kids.

"Maybe he went into the tunnel? Did the kids you work with mention him? He was wearing a school uniform, and he didn't come home. He's a good boy." She paused for a long moment and then continued as if to herself, "I don't know why he left. I remember he was talking about the tunnel . . ."

We told her that we had not heard anything about him, but would show the photo around and take some of her posters up to Tucson.

"Could you take my photo?" She wanted to leave no stone unturned. "If you could take it and if others see it—maybe . . ."

So she posed against a wall there, close by the tunnel entrance, holding up before her the poster of her lost child: a strangely still portrait of fear and loss on the border.

FIVE

LLEGA ROSA / ROSA ARRIVES

E l Boston is in prison. Nobody seems to know where. They
say he was arrested for assault in Tucson and that he is in
for ten years, but nobody is sure of that either," Ramona
told us only moments after warmly welcoming Maeve and me back for
another summer on the border.

We sank into the sofa. I did not know with whom to be angry, so
I was angry with everyone—from those associated with Mi Nueva
Casa to the forces of world capitalism to Boston. And, of course, with
myself. Whatever I had done, whatever I had been to him, had not
been enough. I had written a few short letters since the last summer, sending them through Mi Nueva Casa. He had not answered, but
had—I was told—been happy to receive them, so I had thought that
we could continue where we had left off. I had also dared to believe
in the possibility of a slow but total transformation of Boston's life.
He would learn more and more to express himself through writing
and film, which would give him the motivation to finish school. And
so on. I had not underestimated the forces working against any such
change, but I certainly had an exaggerated idea of my own influence
and had entertained visions, hopes, and illusions. They were gone

now. We later made every effort to locate Boston in the endless maze of Arizona federal prisons into which he very likely had entered with a false name, but we simply could not find him.

"Lorenzo." I looked up to see Flor calling my name. It was strange to see her without Davidcito; she seemed smaller. That was the other big change, but one we had heard about when it happened. Mexican social services had intervened, and Flor had lost custody of Davidcito to her own sister Myrna. It wasn't difficult to see the wisdom in that decision. Certainly the baby was better off in the little cottage in Los Tapiros than in Jesús' shack—*la casita*—where the kids were still hanging out. We nevertheless worried for Flor, not only because she clearly loved her baby, but also because he provided the one constant sense of responsibility in the otherwise shifting chaos of her life. For the others as well, there was no doubt that Davidcito's presence had helped make Barrio Libre a family. What would they be now? I wondered, looking into Flor's soft young face.

When Maeve walked in moments later, Flor ran up and threw her arms about her, sobbing. Maeve cried, too. "Why are we crying?" Maeve asked her, and Flor said, "Because we are happy—happy to see one another! And you should see Davidcito! He's big, very big, and *muy guapo*—very handsome!"

"And Jesús?" I asked. "Where is he?" We had also heard that they were still an item.

"He's fine," she replied, but noted that his picture was missing from the wall. I laughed, remembering the day in the previous summer when Maeve had brought in large prints of all the kids. They loved them, arguing over who was the best looking, asking for copies, and so on. Then Maeve had taken them away to be framed for hanging at Mi Nueva Casa. When she went through them again, she saw that the portrait of Jesús was missing. We suspected he had simply slipped it off the table right before our eyes—a trick for which he was well able. But the other photos had made it onto the walls, and maybe they added a degree of homeliness to the place. At any rate, the kids were clearly delighted not only to look at them, but to use them. As we spoke of one or another kid who had not been there for a while, Flor would point to the pictures of them for the benefit of any newcomers.

At that moment, Jesús himself strode in and, breaking into a huge contented grin, embraced Maeve and gave me the local handshake—open hands slapped together followed by bouncing fists. Still short, he did seem a bit bigger and certainly older than when we had last seen him, and he spoke more coherently.

I told him that he looked good.

"I am not taking paint," he said in response. "I just smoke a little," he grinned. "But no paint."

As we spoke, many of the others arrived. There were some new kids, such as a pair of young brothers recently come from Guadalajara, but mainly our old friends from the previous year—Negro, Chamuco, Chito, David.

We all chatted through lunch. They argued about what had really happened to Boston. Of Guanatos, who had never returned to Mi Nueva Casa from his trip to Guadalajara, they all claimed ignorance.

"Do you want to come up to the casita?" Jesús asked after lunch, so we left, everyone who could pile into my car for the journey bumping through the streets of Nogales, if anything even more crammed with people, cars, and life than it had been the year before. Up in Colonia Los Virreyes, nothing appeared to have changed. The small Catholic Church was no closer to completion that when we had left it, and Jesús' shack was the same tar-papered little square.

But as we approached the doorway, a hand emerged from the inside, sweeping aside the drape that hung there, and a sly-eyed, slight woman of uncertain age emerged to greet us. Her face, dark and sun cracked under a pile of yellow-streaked hair, broke into a gold-toothed smile of greeting. With her matching large hoop earrings, she could have passed for a Gypsy if only she had been wearing a flowing skirt and not tight jeans.

"This is my mother," Jesús explained, "Rosa."

"Pase," she said, waving me into the dark interior. By comparison with the year before, the casita was almost homey. A cast-iron bed had been placed along one wall and another smaller one across from it. At the back, a chest of drawers overflowed with articles of clothing. Over it hung a framed portrait of her son, Jesús—the portrait that had disappeared from the table at Mi Nueva Casa before it could be hung with the others.

jesús

"Nice photo," I said to Jesús, who was standing at my side. He beamed, only slightly sheepish. "Maybe Mah-aye-ba [Maeve] can make another one for my father," he said; it was the first time he had referred to him.

The other walls were decorated with small religious pictures, advertisements snipped from magazines, and greeting card tributes to their mother from Jesús and his younger siblings, whom I could now make out, through the gloom, sitting in the corner.

"This is my brother, Alonzo," Jesús said, presenting a dark-haired delicate boy of maybe thirteen—already his own height. Behind him were two small children: a scrawny, dirt-smeared boy of five with dusty blond hair and a winning grin whom they called Gordo—Fatty, which may have been sarcastic or a reference to an earlier state—and his sister Francesca, a year or so older, who floated shyly to my side. She looked up at me with open curiosity and, when I greeted her, laid a hand softly on my arm.

Alonzo went over to a makeshift kitchen near the doorway—a small table covered with dirty plates and mugs—to pour plastic tumblers of Pepsi. The cooking, I could see, was done outside on a stove made from a rusted oil drum, a standard appliance in this part of the world.

"Sit, sit," Rosa beckoned.

I did, and she explained that she had shown up in Nogales from Imuris a few months earlier. That town, which lay only forty or so miles through dry ranch land to our south, I knew well.

"I have come here to look after my children," she said. "These are with me here; I have another girl down in Magdalena; and there are two others, my eldest boys, who are married. One lives here in Las Brisas." That was another *colonia* in Nogales—another family fact Jesús had never mentioned.

"I am responsible for my children; they need me, and I must take care of them," she said grandly. She passed a card over for my inspection.

"See, that is a card from a *fábrica*—a *maquila*—that says I can work there."

Jesús looked proud. His friends, however, had remained outside, where they were just visible sipping sodas in a narrow band of shade on the side of the shack. I nodded appreciatively and told her that Maeve, whom she knew had taken the portrait of Jesús, and I had returned to work with the kids at Mi Nueva Casa.

"Bueno," she said, but then frowned. "It is good that you are trying to help the kids. Jesús tells me that you take them swimming. Mah-aye-ba teaches them how to take photos. That's good. But Mi Nueva Casa, what does it do for them? They will never change. You know why? Because if they don't force them to change, they won't. They have a shelter there, a place to stay, and they have school, everything, but *es como darles más alas*—it's as if they give them wings. I hear them talking. They say, 'We go there, we shower, we eat, and we just fool around in the school.' Yes, because I have heard them! And that's how they keep going wrong. If only they could stay there in Guaymas. There they have something for the kids, a real detox place. There are two kids who were here in the tunnel, and they got treatment there."

She looked over at her son Alonzo. "I put him in the program there. The doctor told me that if he continues, he will lose his mind. But he doesn't listen to me. I have tried. I took him to Guaymas, but he was so desperate for the drugs that he came back here to Nogales. He does mostly paint."

"And another thing about Mi Nueva Casa," she was on a roll now. "That *licenciado* [professional] they have there, he said to Flor, 'Oh, you look so good in a miniskirt,' and he asked another little girl, 'Do you have any tattoos on your body?' He doesn't have the right to ask that. Flor told me this, and the other girl, too. To me, this is bad, wrong. Why don't they do something for the kids to take them off drugs? We're too poor, and the kids are poor, so why don't they do something for them? There's a lot of badness in the world!"

Of course, I had said the very same things to myself on many occasions.

"And can you do nothing yourself?" I asked.

"I try, but I am not strong enough."

She was probably right, I thought, and wondered whether the home she was trying to make in the shack could move things in a better direction. But how did these changes fit into Barrio Libre? Had Rosa in effect taken away their "clubhouse"?

I told Rosa that I had brought a friend to help at Mi Nueva Casa, a young Mexican man who played guitar and could give lessons to the kids. I suggested that because they all liked music, the guitar might give them a new and better focus. She smiled and agreed. Suddenly enthusiastic for the transforming power of art, I suggested that we could have a fiesta there in the shack the next evening and that I could bring my friend to provide the music. Everyone seemed delighted with the idea, and I bid good-bye and headed off, back to the border to discuss the situation with Maeve and the guitarist, Ricardo.

The next afternoon at Mi Nueva Casa I saw Romel's girlfriend, La Fanta, for the first time since our return. When we left, she was a strikingly beautiful sixteen-year-old mother of a toddler, pregnant with her second child, and, as she had told me in the pool, still a regular in the tunnel. But from what I had heard from Ramona and Loida, she looked to be a possible success story—at least in terms of what we dared expect. Not only was she out of the tunnel, Ramona told me, but she was also off drugs and going to a special school to learn the beautician's craft. She and Romel were still a couple, and in fact they and her two young children were sleeping in a wrecked car outside her mother's home in Colonia Solidaridad. She came to the Casa after school every day, usually bringing the baby but leaving her older daughter with her own mother in Solidaridad.

"Romel is still a problem," Loida told me. "She is trying to get him to be responsible, but he is very lazy."

When Fanta strode in, the baby perching on her hip and her toddler tripping behind, Ramona leaned over to me and whispered, "And she is Vero—Verónica—now. She doesn't want to be called Fanta."

"Hola, Lorenzo," she nearly purred, kissing me on the cheek and holding up the baby for my inspection. Vero had put on about twenty pounds, but was still a knock-out, her natural beauty now enhanced by the careful grooming she was no doubt learning at the school. The girls, Sayra and Mayra, were as beautiful as their mother, though with lighter skin and jet black hair. The oldest was nearly four now, and the baby Mayra was four months. She was Romel's and looked like

ROMEL, VERO (LA FANTA), AND MAYRA

him—a fact Vero was delighted to have me confirm, laughing and
thrusting her into my hands.

I asked her about the school, and she told me that it was great,
that she was learning a lot and was the best in her class. I promised
we would visit her there. She asked for Maeve, and I told her that she
returned as well and would be doing more photos. Vero turned to look
at the portraits then and told me in her usual blunt, almost aggressive manner that she did not like the placement of her own photo.

"I don't want to be next to that bitch," she said referring to Flor.
"We are not friends."

I asked her what had happened, and she recounted a fragmentary
tale, the gist of which was that Flor owed her two hundred pesos they
had obtained some months earlier in the tunnel—from a robbery,
I suspected, no doubt before her reformation. Anyway, she insisted
that the placement of the photos reflect their current enmity.

I changed the subject, and we joined Ramona, Loida, and Maeve,
who had arrived with her cameras, for a late snack. Afterward, Vero
invited us to give her and her daughters a ride to her home.

Solidaridad was one of the larger new colonias that every day pushed
the edge of the city farther into the surrounding desert. It was a series of steep round hills of yellow dirt, pushed and piled into looping
paths and roads, and studded with a nearly infinite variety of homes.
These homes ranged from the substantial brick-walled, satellite-
dished bases of minor drug lords to a series of tacked wooden boxes,
like the one where Vero and her extended, perhaps overextended,
family lived. From Vero's home, we could see far and wide across this
newly peopled landscape. Clearly, such a view—bought at the price of
distance from the few meager services—is not a valued commodity.
The poorest people perch atop these loose sand mountains, living in
houses built of scraps until they can afford to buy sheets of heavy-
duty cardboard, plywood, or—if they entertain visions of snug family
futures—cinder blocks. Vero's mother María asked us to sit on some of
those very blocks, which extended westward from the shack to form a
still low enclosure, hoping to rise into the walls of a modest, but solid
home.

"You see," María explained, "when you have some money, you buy as many of these blocks as you can, and you put down a row, or a few rows. Otherwise you will blow it away on a fiesta or something. This way you build when you can, and eventually you finish the house. This one will cost maybe fifteen hundred dollars. It will take a while."

If it is ever finished, I thought, once again surveying the view and noting the dozens of such construction projects that surrounded us. I suppose that one could see these projects as a hopeful sign, the mark of an area that, however poor, had some work and where there was enough money at least to begin building more substantial homes. Or else one might see in them the tragedy of so many as-pirations that would never be fulfilled, of homes and families that would collapse in on themselves long before enough resources could be assembled to build a larger, more commodious life.

I looked at María, a round, dark woman somewhere in her thirties, and wondered how and when the money would be found to realize her modest dream. Her mate, a minor *coyote* according to Vero, had clearly been the best hope of finding that sum of money, but he had been in a U.S. jail for some months, and no one seemed to know when he was getting out. María herself worked in one of the maquiladoras when she could. With five of her own children, the youngest two of whom were under five, however, making arrangements to work was not easy. It was a good walk even to the closest stop of the battered minivans—private capillaries on the public circulation system—that would take her to a bus that would, in turn, take her to the industrial parks on the farthest edges of the city. Looking for work was trying enough. Showing up on time every day from these outposts meant major hassles, and the wages, if she could get them, would never leave much for cinder blocks.

"Sometimes my sister works, and I look after her children, and sometimes it goes the other way." Her sister Lupe in fact lived right next door in a nearly identical shack leaning into María's. They had come up together from Empalme, just outside of Guaymas, some years earlier, but had lived in Solidaridad for only two years. Lupe had no man. Her oldest child was Jesús, "Negro" as I knew him in Barrio Libre, a name that referred to his very dark Indian complexion. He

EL NEGRO

was someone I saw frequently but of whom I knew little. At Mi Nueva Casa, he was lethargic to the point of being comatose. On the street, he was equally quiet, but alert and wary, as he was when we had arrived at Vero's that afternoon, peering at us over a broken wall like a silent lizard while the little children—Lupe's, María's, and Vero's—had swarmed happily about our legs, leading us up the broken rock-and-dirt "stairway" to their homes. Now Negro found a place on the wall just down from us, still quiet but apparently at ease, stroking the sorry-looking yellow hound that huffed in the shade by his feet.

Vero was busy with her two girls, nursing tiny Mayra and alternately embracing and bellowing at the toddler Sayra, who dodged about with the other kids, pushing and laughing on the edge of an empty cistern.

"When we get the water, it will go in here," Vero said, making it serve as a bench for the present. "And Romel and I will have a room there," she motioned toward one weedy corner of the square of dirt enclosed by two tiers of cinder blocks. She smiled as I filmed the enclosure with the video camera. I was looking at the wrecked car on the slope below, where this family of four was sleeping in the meantime, when Vero said brightly, "Have you seen Romel's chicken? You can film that, too! And Mah-aye-ba can take photos!"

Vero led us into her mother's shack, where Romel was napping on a narrow bunk bed.

"Romel, show them the chicken. Lorenzo and Mah-aye-ba can take pictures!"

Romel rose groggily from his bed and saluted us with a sleepy grin and the Barrio Libre handshake. Like Boston in some ways, he was the best and the worst of the kids. His experience in the United States and the ups and downs with a drug-dealing father had made his life even a bit more complicated and varied than the others'. Perhaps those movements and dislocations had made Romel reflective. He always seemed more self-conscious and more aware of the larger world in which he operated—making him very interesting to be with sometimes, but very difficult at others. Once, the director of Mi Nueva Casa, seeing potential, had decided to make Romel a kind of assistant. "You will be sorry," Romel had said, laughing softly but quite serious. "I am going to fuck things up." He had paused and looked into the director's eyes. "I will fuck things up, and that's for sure." Sometimes he was the most adult of all of them, nearly eighteen and looking very much the professional minor criminal—an expert leader and robber of would-be immigrants in the tunnel. That same sense of responsibility, we hoped, might be used to make things work with Vero and the kids, especially now that she at least was out of the tunnel, in school, and purportedly off drugs. He seemed proud of his baby Mayra, but he was prone to lying about for many hours at a time. Ramona and Loida were convinced that he was simply and deeply lazy. He might have been, but his circumstances would have overwhelmed my own resolve, that's certain. He was, after all, the eighteen-year-old partner to a flamboyant, determined girl with two little children; he had a grade-school education and no prospects beyond the tunnel. Strong ambition, if he had it, would lead only to more lucrative—and dangerous—criminal activities.

But Vero knew another side of him—they all did—and now they wanted us to see the "chicken" that shared their dark and airless shack. Across from the bunk beds were two more beds, each a thin mattress sinking into a metal frame. Everywhere were pieces of clothing and general debris. A huge American basketball poster covered a refrigerator by the doorway, and the portrait of a Mexican soccer player adorned a rickety wardrobe. Romel pulled a carton from under the bottom bunk bed and plunked it down on one of the beds across the room. Everyone sat on the other.

"Here she is," Romel said quietly, looking up at us with tender pride. "She's got some eggs." We all leaned over the box and peered in as if it were the Baby of Bethlehem. With great tenderness, Romel nudged his hand under the quaking bird, shifting her slightly and revealing the gleam of soft white eggshells beneath. "Take her photo," he said.

Maeve did.

"Take the baby with the video now," Lupe said, motioning toward Vero's Mayra. "Now Sayra," another child added. "Now this one. Now that one." The kids fell over each other in a frenzy—not to be filmed themselves, but to make sure their younger brothers and sisters were.

A typical Mexican scene, I thought, for I had seldom been anywhere in the country that people were not anxious to have photos taken and displayed. No home I had visited there, no matter how humble, lacked a photo of children. María's was no exception. The wall behind the bed was made of sheets of cardboard stapled in overlapping layers. On it was a framed set of no fewer than six portraits of one of her children. Another's face was photographically emblazoned on the face of a nonfunctioning wall clock. In the euphoria of this infinite regress of representation, the kids demanded that I film the still photos on the wall.

When I had done all that, I played the tape back to universal delight. We watched it on the little screen of the video camera, four or five kids climbing over my shoulders or sneaking under my arms. Romel and Vero were more jaded and strolled outside, but Vero's mother and aunt, María and Lupe—looking like two round teen friends at a sleep-over—fell on the bed in spasms of laughter and joy, making me promise to return to show them more on another occasion.

Before leaving, while Maeve chatted with María about the trials of motherhood, I took time to look out over the colonia again, to see it in the declining, soft golden evening. In that light, everything appears prettier, softer, and less washed out by the cruel white of the desert noon, but also dirtier. The layers, streaks, and tears are visible on every object and person. But this time I was most struck by the tires—big truck tires everywhere, for here, as elsewhere in the third world, tires are endlessly recycled building materials. Much of Colonia Solidaridad was in fact propped up by tires, which, when filled with sand, formed the most solid ground, buttressing the edge of otherwise sliding sand hills. Or they could be arranged upright in decorative fences, laid atop houses to hold down roofs, or simply allowed to find their own enigmatic positions up and down the rises and gullies. In the slantwise light of the early evening, these cast-off tires gleamed like a thousand jewel-like ponds, for windblown plastic bags had found them, and each held rain water from the last brief summer shower. An excellent breeding ground for mosquitoes, I thought, but beautiful all the same.

Vero was suddenly at my elbow, and I remembered to tell her about the fiesta that night at the casita in nearby Virreyes. "Rosa seems to have improved the place," I ventured.

She looked at me as if I were the most naive, benighted innocent imaginable.

"She sends them all out to rob and get her drugs. She takes drugs with all of them, and she is fucking all of Jesús' friends." She sneered, "She'd fuck Romel, too, if I let him hang around there!"

Despite Vero's warnings, I went to see *la familia Rosa* later that night. As promised, I brought along Ricardo and his guitar for the fiesta. "Poor Vero," I thought as we entered, for the first person I made out in the gloom was Romel, stretched out on a bed again, but this time in a glassy-eyed trance. He could barely raise his hand in greeting. Across the room was Jesús' brother Alonzo, holding up to his face a can of Coke, from which he appeared to be taking frequent, shallow sips. But I knew enough by then to recognize that movement as another way in which to inhale spray paint. There was another can on the floor beside Romel.

Jesús and a girl I did not know looked sober enough, however, and welcomed us in. Rosa was fixed up and almost pretty in the dim light. Alonzo and Francesca were sent to the shop and returned with a great sack of soda and potato chips. Ricardo played, and we all sang—Romel, too, from the bed. Rosa and I danced while little Gordo and Francesca ran and spun around us as if this gathering were any happy family party.

"Lorenzo, Lorenzo!" It was Negro and Chito, who had just arrived, bursting into the shack, faces wild and clothes streaked with muck. "It's Guanatos!" they shouted. "He's been arrested. You must find him and visit him!"

"So he is back from Guadalajara," I said, stating the obvious.

"He came just this week," Chito said. "They arrested him coming out of the tunnel, Los Vampiros. Betas took him."

"What was he doing?" I asked.

"Nothing! Nothing!" they insisted. "We had just come back from visiting on the other side. We were already up, and Guanatos was just coming out when some Betas jumped down and grabbed him. They said he had assaulted someone, but he hadn't. Really. You must find him and see him."

So we did, Maeve and I, but it was not easy. We spent the next morning going from office to office, first just to find out where he was and what sort of charge was against him.

"Here he is," a friendly woman was finally able to tell us, having searched a number of lists of the recently arrested. "He was arrested yesterday for assault in the tunnel. He's in the municipal jail until the trial. You can visit him there if you like." She explained that because Guanatos was now eighteen, he faced a real sentence if convicted.

The front room of the jail was dank enough, but the gloom beyond, where corridors disappeared around frightening corners, seemed designed to induce a hopeless depression. We stood waiting by the counter, listening to a young man's voice crying shrilly for his mother again and again. Suddenly, the guard appeared and approached us.

"Can I be of service?" he said, smiling with the grace of a maître d' showing us to the best table in a restaurant. We explained who we were and that we had hoped to see Guanatos. Still smiling, he leaned over one edge of the counter and drew back a sliding shutter, revealing a set of black bars and an impenetrable gloom beyond. He called our friend's name, and we waited till Guanatos's face loomed into view like the ghost of Achilles. He pressed a deeply tanned, dirt-stained face against the bars and stretched a filth-blackened hand through them. Incredibly, he was smiling—an angelic, dimpled martyr.

"Lorenzo, Mah-aye-ba," he whispered. He was on the edge of tears, and so were we. The fear and revulsion I had first felt gave way to an unbearably heavy sadness. He said he had done nothing, that he had been arrested without cause. The guard, who was still standing by the counter, looked as if he neither believed nor disbelieved. We told Guanatos that we would find out what we could, and then we spoke of other things—of Guadalajara and his trip there. He had seen his family and decided to stay for a while, but after some months without many prospects, he had returned to the border.

"I am staying with Tío, at the *llantera* [tire repair place] just a few blocks from the Stupid Dummy. He gives me a place to sleep and some work." He then asked for news of the others, and we spoke of Jesús and Flor, Vero and Romel, and of everyone's prospects. Finally, the guard nodded, indicating our time was up, and without ceremony slid shut the wood panel, cutting off Guanatos and returning us to the still-green gloom of the room.

six ¿De dónde eres? / Where Are You From?

"¿De dónde eres?" "Where are you from?"

t is a question any Mexican would ask, of course. Or any Irishman, Frenchman, or American. It is a way of establishing a connection, a relation. Do you know that place? Have you been there? It is also a search for an identity, a way of asking who you are. In the United States, we often ask "What do you do?" in order to find out who somebody is. For most Mexicans, place still comes well before occupation. Guanatos and Chito always said *mi tierra,* "my land," "my territory," "my home"—something of all that in a place where you are still supposed to stay rooted, even if many do not.

"Where are you from?" It was the only one of Boston's questions that concerned the past, so you might think that the kids lived totally in a kind of Nogales street present. But you would be wrong. Though they were cast adrift, all of these kids were from somewhere, and, like all Mexicans, most of them talked about the place of their birth and of their parents'. La Flor could not remember anything about the town she left as an infant but would say with pride in its fabled beaches, "I am from Puerto Peñasco." Even those who had left

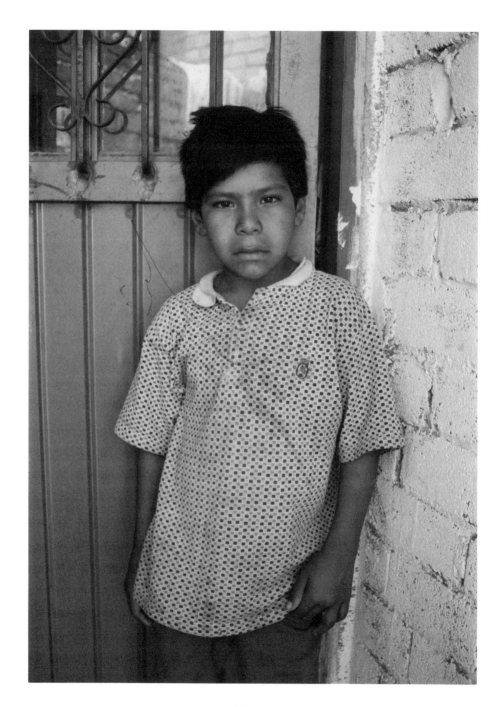

DIEGO

their tierra in bitter disappointment seemed proud of the land from which they came. That was certainly true of those who had come from the state of Jalisco and its principal city, Guadalajara, from whence there seems to be a regular flow to the border. Both Romel, who had left it at the age of nine for the United States, and El Boston, another child refugee from there, would speak approvingly of the regional attractions. Guanatos, of course, was a particular Jalisco chauvinist, singing its songs and tearfully remembering its many churches. It was as if they did not come from god-forsaken slums somewhere on the city's boundless periphery. But most of the kids were from the north, *puro Sonora* they like to say: Chito and his pal Armando were from Navojoa, and many of the kids—La Fanta, El Negro, Chiguile, El Chamuco—came with their families from Empalme, near Guaymas.

Chango ("Monkey")—whose real name was Ernesto—was also a Sonorense, but from the south of the state, and he wanted to go home.

"You are going to Guaymas?" he asked me in his hushed but rapid mumble. We had just arrived for the day at Mi Nueva Casa and had not had time to put down our cameras.

"I might soon, yes," I replied.

Chango had been coming to the casa for only a few days, arriving at the door before it opened at 9:00 A.M., a reliable sign that he was sleeping on the street or in the tunnel. He was skinnier, dirtier, and more ragged than the other kids, and he often had the shakes, so I was not surprised when he told me that he had been taking heroin but had been trying to quit for several days. Trying to kick the habit while living in the streets is not easy, though, and in me he perhaps saw a way out.

"If you took me there," his eyes were wide with a kind of frantic hope, "I could get home to Obregón. It's only another couple of hours after Guaymas. I haven't seen my mother for three years, more . . . it's hard here for me . . ." His voice fell below my hearing then, but his liquid eyes were focused on the possibility of a return to *su tierra y su familia*.

In fact, I had been thinking about going down to Guaymas to see how Rosa, Jesús' mother, was doing. I must admit that when I first met him, I found Jesús difficult to like. He seemed an aggressive, stupid, ugly little character—nearly always hopped up on drugs and often difficult at Mi Nueva Casa: starting fights, stealing food, and so on. I couldn't see why Flor would be attracted to him. But as we came to know one another over that first summer, I slowly saw another Jesús emerge. Perhaps he felt the same about me. In this second summer, especially since I had met his mother, Jesús and I had become much closer. When he was with La Flor—the Flower—they seemed to me almost the star-crossed lovers of myth and story. They were a dark miniature—two lithe figures entwined in embrace or more often leaning into one another as they searched the surrounding world for friends and enemies.

What was most difficult to understand was Jesús' relation with his mother Rosa. He showed no sign of knowing what she was evidently up to with his friends. Guanatos in particular had become her regular consort since his release from jail two days after our visit (the alleged victim had not shown up in court). Rosa was even occasionally described by the others as his *novia*—girlfriend. In her unpredictable jumps between queen of the den of iniquity and desperate mother of five minors, she had evidently taken herself and the little ones off suddenly to Guaymas and the Casa San Franciscana, a shelter run by the Franciscan brothers but with some connection to the Mexican children's welfare organization, Desarrollo Integral de la Familia (DIF). Jesús had shown me a wrinkled scrap of paper on which his mother had printed some words in a crooked, shaky hand: the name of the place and the phrase "we eat and stay there."

"They can stay there for two weeks," he had told me. "The Franciscans will give them a piece of land, and my mother can build a little house, better than the casita in Los Virreyes." It seemed far too good to be true—first that the Franciscans had land to give away and even more so that his mother, Doña Rosa, would emerge long enough from her habitual drugged haze to organize such an effort. Anyway, it seemed a good opportunity to see Jesús' family trying to do something or at least making the motions.

So Jesús had told Chango about the possible trip, and now he wanted to go, and Chiguile, too, who had come to Mi Nueva Casa with Chango that morning.

"I am from Empalme—right there next to Guaymas, so I too would like to go."

Irresistible requests, and in Chango's case, it seemed unlikely that he could be worse off anywhere else. When I said yes, that we would go the next day, Saturday, Chango and Chiguile nearly burst with excitement.

"We'll go tell Jesús!"

I began the next morning as usual, rousting my assistant, Ricardo. He had spent another night playing guitar and draining liters of Pacifico on his friend's rooftop, high in one of the old, cobbled-street neighborhoods in the center of the city. As I waited for him to emerge from the shattered chaos of an apartment that he had not cleaned since it had been burglarized and trashed once again a couple of weeks earlier, I wondered about the wisdom of having hired him. In many ways, though, Ricardo was perfect for the job of guide-assistant. I had needed someone who knew the city to go around Nogales with me and catch any of the kids' rapid, slurred Spanish that I missed. Not that Ricardo was bodyguard material; he was half my size, a skinny guy with a haggard mop of black curls who could have passed for any kind of Mediterranean—Spanish, Italian, or Jewish like me. In fact, he reminded me of my own brother. He was completely *fronterizo*, though, born in Mexico City but partially educated in California, and residing for most of his life within a few hundred yards of either side of the Nogales border. He gave guitar lessons to poor kids on both sides of the border. As he liked to explain whenever a border guard asked him about the guitar, "These kids are going to meet each other one day. Would you rather they be carrying knives and guns or guitars?"

Ricardo was a great guide; not only did he know the streets, but he also provided music wherever we found ourselves, and the kids liked him—though I think they found him a bit crazy. He was either asleep or nearly spinning and exploding with nervous energy—compulsively picking the Beatles or Bach on "Nina," as he called his guitar. When the day's or evening's work was done, he would head off once again with a shopping bag full of *cahuamas*—brown liter bottles of beer.

Ricardo finally emerged, swallowed his cigarette in five long drags, and dived into the car. He had a hangover but was already happy about the voyage as we drove up to Los Virreyes and Jesús' *casita*.

I was always nervous about what we would find there. Even in the morning, I was conscious of eyes everywhere following our progress by car up the rutted dirt roads and then on foot through a yard strewn with the debris of food, drink, and of course drugs—that is, empty cans of spray paint. But that morning the scene was different. We were only twenty minutes late, and Chango was already there, standing outside with a new *cholo* haircut of short spikes and a rat's tail. His pants were dirty, but only because he had no others to wear. He had managed to wash a shirt and was smiling like a kid about to go off to summer camp. Inside the shack were Chiguile, Jesús, and Flor.

When everyone emerged from the gloom of the casita prepared to travel, I knew we already had a problem. There was room for only three in the backseat. I had not expected Flor. She was the only one with no relations to visit, but she was determined to go with Jesús, not only because she liked the idea of a trip, but also because she was struggling to keep their relationship going. Although they were still an item, there had been hints that all was not well between her and Rosa, her potential mother-in-law. Jesús' attention, as well, had been wandering. He was, of course, the original reason for the trip, and he wasn't going to go without Flor. Chango had become just as central to the journey, so that left Chiguile, who knew it was up to him to "change his mind," so he did.

"I don't want to go," he mumbled.

There were other reasons, too, I think—hints the day before from both Chango and Chiguile about the need for clothes to return in.

Clothes are both themselves and more than themselves. Clothing here—as in so many urban street cultures from New York to Naples—is critical. I thought once again of Boston's question, "Have you always dressed as a cholo?" To be a cholo was to dress like one, and, at

Chiguile

the same time, to have good, new, and clean clothes was the visible
sign—often the only visible sign—of relative success on the streets.
But that success was often fleeting and elusive, so Chiguile had, like
many of these kids, a volatile mixture of pride, shame, and cunning.
In this world, you could beg, but stealing was more honorable. I remembered Chiguile dressing to leave the pool one day, furiously rubbing every scrap of dirt from his white tennies. That same day he
would not ask me for a few pesos for the bus, feigning—or so I had
assumed—the intention to walk home until I had offered to treat
everyone to the bus. He had accepted but, as the bus arrived, had
quietly insisted that I give him the money so that he could enter the
bus last, paying for all of us.

Chiguile may thus well have been afraid, too, ashamed to return
with nothing, of showing up a failure in the eyes of his family and of
the cholos of home.

In any case, when I said that he could come, that we would somehow manage to take everyone, he only became more resolute and de-
pressed. *"No quiero ir"*—"I don't want to go"—was his only answer.
The other three milled around, each with his plastic supermarket bag
of clothes and toiletries (Jesús would not travel without a tiny bottle
of men's cologne). The holiday mood was fading fast in the growing
heat. When we finally left, Chiguile didn't come out to say good-bye.

The kids loved getting under way. Flor and Jesús settled into a
snuggle they would keep up for three days, while Chango seemed to
look more inward than out, probably thinking about what lay ahead
for him. The last traffic lights and Tecate *depósitos* of the city gave
way to the new peripheral roads and industrial parks—now home to
a hundred *maquiladoras*. Then the last dirt city roads fell behind us
and we began to climb and wind over dry grass hills.

"Something is going to happen," Ricardo said suddenly. Then he
paused as if searching the immediate future. "No, nothing very big.
Nothing bigger than a flat tire. Do you have a spare?" He seemed so
sure of this prediction, which he made as if it were simply a report of
the facts, that I believed him but forgot the warning as we made our
way south through about thirty-five miles of hilly, dry ranch lands

framed by scrub-green mountains. There were only patches of settlement until Imuris, a pleasant Sonoran village that the new highway
had cruelly bisected and turned into a busy truck stop. I suggested
we stop for lunch, for Imuris is famous for its *quesadillas,* local cheese
melted between a pair of small flour tortillas, to which you can add
pieces of meat, chilis, salsa, cucumber, and pickled onions. We chose
one of the roadside *taquerías,* a semi-enclosed space with a few plastic tables and chairs behind the open-air brick grill. The pungent
aroma of beef and scallions mixed with the truck fumes. We laughed
at Ricardo's inability to take more than two bites without a chord
from Nina. Finally, with a big platter of those quesadillas under our
belts, we rose to find the birthplace of Jesús, for Imuris was his home.

In fact, we knew we had entered *la tierra de Jesús* as soon as we
descended into the valley some miles from the town. Looking out
over the hills that flanked the road, he said, "There, beyond that
hill lives an uncle, . . . over by the river a grandfather." That commentary would continue through the entire valley of the Río Magdalena.
Jesús' own birth house is no longer "in the family," though. We found
it not far from the river on a dirt road along a large stretch of fallow
fields choked in bristling weeds.

As modest as it was, I couldn't help thinking how much better
looking this simple brick rectangle of three rooms in a row was than
the casita in Los Virreyes, a kind of kids' clubhouse in the dirt. Jesús
wanted to take a picture of it, but of course with himself in the
photo, so Chango took the camera and snapped away. Nobody was
around to mind.

It had been a long time since Jesús had lived in that house. He and
his brothers had been dragged along in a downward spiral that had
led from rural poverty to urban marginality, from the fields of Imuris
to Colonia Los Virreyes, and from alcohol to every sort of drug. He recited the tale as we drove away.

"My father left us two years ago. He fought with my mother because he thought she was going out with someone else; he was very
jealous. My mother wasn't going out like that, but he was an alco-
holic and smoked a lot of marijuana. He would beat my mother

whenever he liked. She would cry. He would come home drunk. My papa would give half of his drugs to my mama. Among us all we managed. We kids washed windshields. We would make more or less six hundred pesos doing that."

Flor was looking at him intently as he continued.

"When we left the house there in Imuris, we found another with one room. We all slept in the same bed. Some slept above and others below. We also had a sofa bed. We had a radio and a television. That place we rented, but then some cholos burned it down. Now we are in the casita, and that is rented, too. We want to build a house, but we can't because we don't have enough to do it. My mother is responsible to take care of us, and so she didn't want to leave her kids alone. That's why she came to us there, and that is why she is down in Guaymas now, trying to get a house for us."

It was the first time that I had heard Jesús speak in that way, calmly reflective on his circumstances. During the previous summer, he had been nearly always quietly drugged, slumping in front of the television or frenetically and aggressively running between rooms at Mi Nueva Casa. It was if the journey—even with his friends—had loosed something in him. He came to life even more as we drove on to the south. He continued to spot relatives, and he began to discuss the features of the human landscape he knew, such as the greenhouses growing flowers, a tiny airport in which one of his brothers had worked. As we entered the town of Magdalena, he pointed out the statues, the great but now tattered and drooping mourning bows, and the graffiti to the fallen local hero, Luis Donaldo Colosio, the presidential candidate from Magdalena who had been assassinated four years before. "He's like the Kennedys," Jesús said. "When he was alive, he wasn't much, but now that he's dead, he's a hero!"

It only seemed right to pull into the town square, as any Sonoran would do, to "go see San Francisco"—that is, the reclining statue of San Francisco Xavier that lies in the mission, receiving a steady stream of pilgrims through the year and thousands during the fiesta of early October. Mexicans always know what to do with a saint, whether or not they have seen a particular version, and these kids were no exception. Jesús had been there before, the others not, but

they all grazed a tender hand over wooden feet, knees, hands, and—
lifting the head as they had seen other pilgrims in the line ahead of
them do—blessed themselves and blew a soft kiss into their hands.

As we left the church, Chango seemed overwhelmed. Putting an
arm on his shoulder, I asked him how he felt. "I don't know," he replied, " a little sad . . . a sadness has come over me . . . I don't know
why." However he was feeling about going home—and God knows his
feelings must have been mixed—San Francisco had brought something bubbling to the surface, something he could think more about
as we continued south, passing through Santa Ana and into the open
desert unbroken for a hundred miles, the road a blue line disappear-
ing into the horizon.

We were approaching the state capital, Hermosillo, when I decided
to take the road through the grape country to avoid a hefty toll. We
had gone only a mile or two when we felt the nauseating wrench of a
wheel dropping into one of the thousands of cavernous potholes that
decorated the "free road." We bumped off into the dirt and piled out
of the car. Before we had everything out of the trunk, a pickup full of
locals pulled over, and we all changed the tire.

Ricardo's prophecy had come true, and he was relieved that nothing more would now happen. "So that's it," he said, "and it's not so
bad really. It is often said that Mexico is a disorganized country, but
you will see that is not so. We have a flat tire, and there will be a
place to fix it within a few hundred meters. Where there are potholes, there are *llanteras;* that is the beauty of our national aptitude
for organization."

Llanteras are the ubiquitous tire shops that are a kind of third
world institution. I am not talking about Mr. Goodyear or Michelin,
but rather anything from one enterprising youth sitting in the shade
to a sun-bleached shack and ramada manned by an entire family. In
any case, they will be equipped with massive iron hand tools and
piles of used tires, every one of which would be deemed in need of
changing by any American service station. Ricardo was right again.
We hadn't gone more than six hundred yards on the tiny "donut"
spare when a llantera loomed into view. "You see," Ricardo remarked

laughing. "Forget about Germany. Mexico is in fact the most systematic country." A further element in the system was the café just next door. We drank our sodas and listened to tapes of Los Tigres del Norte while a young man, wielding what looked like iron-age tools, replaced our shattered tire with one intact but already worn smooth by tens of thousands of miles on Mexican roads. He didn't dare bang the dented rim back into shape, though. *"El calor* [the heat]," he said, showing us another wheel on which such an operation had been attempted: below the dent, a deep fissure had finished off the rim. So we had no choice but to try it as it was and in fact managed only about ten miles when the second tire exploded. Back on with the donut and south to Guaymas and the Casa San Franciscana.

The shelter was locked, but a number of kids and adults were standing in the evening light, waiting for the padre in charge to return and open the gate. He arrived, a mute priest in flowing white robes, and assured us with distant gestures that there would be space for all three kids, so we left them and headed into the seamy nightlife of Guaymas.

We returned to the shelter the next morning to find not only Jesús, Flor, and Chango, but also Jesús' mother, Rosa, three of his younger siblings, and two of her possible teen lovers, Jorge (El Chamuco) and our old friend Guanatos.

We greeted each warmly, and then I turned to look at Rosa, wondering about her plans. Would Guaymas be any better than Nogales? It was prettier. Palm trees lined the highway, and only a few hundred yards from the shelter, the fabulous harbor lined with shrimp boats opened onto nearly oriental green cones of mountains and the blue Sea of Cortez beyond. A lively crowd swarmed downtown, and the women—or so it seemed to Ricardo and me—smiled more than in Nogales. But there were plenty of poor people here, too, of course, and less work, as everybody agreed. The town had fewer *maquilas,* and those that were there offered lower pay.

"We have been washing windshields here," Guanatos told me—one of the bottom-rung enterprises with which it is always possible to make a temporary living if there is enough traffic, but not enough to make you want to stay. As for the free land from the padres, on that subject there was the swirling confusion I had expected. Rosa maintained that such land was available, but the Franciscans themselves told me that they had nothing of the sort. At any rate, the sudden appearance of my car there in Guaymas was generally taken as another option, and now they all wanted to leave—hoping that somehow I would get six more people into the little Geo Prism to go back to Nogales. I explained that we were still on our way south to Obregón and Chango's family, so Ricardo, Chango, Flor, Jesús, and I climbed into the car, and we left the others on the sidewalk happily considering the possibilities of jumping a train.

We headed further south through increasingly humid lands, eventually reaching the rural outskirt of Ciudad Obregón, not so romantically called Barrio Yaqui Dos—Number Two Yaqui Barrio.

The settlement was actually a series of small adobe houses ranged along irrigation canals that brought water from the Río Yaqui to those dry lands. Now it was thick with huge fields of chilies and other vegetable crops that began almost immediately behind the houses and stretched for miles until the land rose abruptly upward in the sierra wall.

Chango's home was much like all the others, a white-washed adobe box with a tin roof. The yard, again like all the others, was an uneven, scrubby dirt patch with a few trees for much-needed shade, a small coop—although the chickens seemed to run free—a large dog tied to a tree, and a shaggy sway-backed horse grazing in the rough grass.

As soon as we pulled up, curious children and more wary adults began to peer at us from behind doorways and trees, but when we dismounted and Chango was visible, everyone came up to meet him. Chango's eyes, however, were looking back down the dirt road we had just traveled, at a steady column of dust. It turned out to be a taxi, rumbling toward us on the narrow dirt road alongside the irrigation canal. We were still scattered awkwardly about the side of the road like the distracted characters in some rock video. Ricardo stood squinting into the sunlight and clutching his guitar case; Flor and Jesús crouched by the canal, staring across at a boy who was about to walk his horse down the steep slope to a bath in the flowing brown water. I was reaching into the car, fumbling for the video camera. Chango must have known who was arriving because as he stared down the road, his dark, flat face twitched into a nervous smile.

Chango's mother climbed heavily out of the taxi with an armful of groceries, followed by a younger, lean man, shirtless under a large cowboy hat. She stopped to look at her prodigal son, then at all of us, then at him again in quiet disbelief. Small wonder. As she later told us, she had not seen her son in nearly two years, and now he was suddenly back, in the company of a motley crew of complete strangers— a bearded American; a young, hot-wired, skinny Mexican man with a guitar; and a pair of cholo lovers leaning into one another at the side of the canal.

When she recovered herself, Chango's mother embraced him and, turning to the rest of us, introduced herself as Isabel. Two young girls were sent to fetch chairs, and we all sat down under a large cottonwood tree, surrounded by a dozen or so children—among them a sweet little girl wearing a soiled communion dress and carrying an infant. Isabel told us that the children were family and friends, from theirs and the surrounding homes. She was herself born in the house and had never left the barrio.

"My mother is from Mobas, my father Nuri, villages high in the sierra."

Yaqui Indian villages, I presumed, and asked her.

"Yes," she answered. "All these came down here from the Yaqui villages there," she said, gazing for a moment toward the ragged brown peaks to our east. "My parents speak Yaqui; I understand it, and these," she said looking at the children, "know only very few words."

While she was talking, Isabel pulled a toddler onto her lap and began stroking him like a lapdog. The little girl in the communion dress filled an old wooden bucket with water and began to wash the infant in it. Two bright-eyed teenage girls crowded into a seat next to Chango and began to examine the small tattoo on his forearm, the three dots that stand for *"mi vida loca"*—my crazy life—a symbol that identified him as a member of Barrio Libre. Two boys of about seventeen, dressed as cholos in oversize pants and long, sleeveless white T-shirts, wandered over and found seats next to Ricardo and me.

Isabel spoke, looking over at the girls.

"What is there here for them? There is almost no work. These ones are picking chilies now for forty pesos a day—about five dollars. At most they make forty-five. Do you see? They get paid two pesos for each *cubeta* of chilies they pick, but the produce owners decide whether to pay by the bucket or by the day. If there are a lot of chilies, it's by the day; if few, by the bucket." Everyone laughed with resignation. "There are not many now," one of the girls told us, "so we gave up after half the day and have made less than twenty pesos." The chickens ran between our legs, so I asked whether they planted anything themselves. "No," Isabel answered, "we haven't enough land for that . . . just the chickens."

"And this one," for the first time she dared to fix her eyes on Chango, who was sitting bolt upright looking like a shy, well-behaved twelve year old throughout, "I don't know if he is staying or leaving. *Se fue escondido*—he left in secrecy, early in the morning. He said nothing. No good-bye."

"I'm staying," Chango whispered.

"Why did he leave?" Ricardo asked Isabel.

"I will tell you the truth!" she answered. "Because he likes *la vagoncía*—delinquency. Because if he liked it here at home, at home he would have stayed."

"His older brother," she continued after a pause, "is crazier than this one. He lives with his aunt. He is even more lost than Chango; he'll use anything that gets into his hands." She was almost teary as she spoke, but looked hopeful. Her boyfriend paced in the background, smiling at us but saying nothing. Then one of Chango's sisters arrived with a beautifully arranged platter of *doridos*—deep fried tacos—and bottles of Pepsi. The two boys that had sat beside me got my attention and asked how much clothing costs in Nogales. "Because it's real expensive here." They were gathering border intelligence, as Chango must have done in his turn.

We began to tell them about the life of the border, thinking we were painting a desperate picture, but the more we said, the more interested these rural cholos seemed, and even Isabel said, "Oh, so the people over there have a lot of stuff!" She was thinking about Chango again and continued without looking at him, "He would have had the chance to work in the fields or in Obregón—on construction, though that is too hard for the kids. He knows the jobs that we have here."

If her depiction of work in the fields wasn't attractive, her portrait of the streets of Obregón was no more so.

"A lot of kids go to Obregón to wash windshields, to hang out. There's a mountain of wild kids there; they make themselves crazy on drugs, and they get into vice more and more. Eventually they just take off, or they get caught. The police pick up the kids constantly. It's sure money for them. Every time they pick up one of mine I have to go bail him out, borrowing fifty, sixty, up to a hundred pesos. Often there are no charges, no nothing. They do their drugs in front of people; the police come and take them, search them, and take their *mota* for themselves. And when they get to the station, they add charges, like robbery or whatever."

"They think we are rats," said one of the boys next to me. "They get confused because we dress cholo style, but we are not thieves. We dress like this to go to dances."

Isabel stared toward the canal, patting her knee and constantly checking on the younger children, who were watching the girl in the communion dress bring the newly bathed infant to Chango. "Say hello to your little nephew," his mother said to him. "He was born long after you left."

We thanked Isabel for her hospitality, and she us for having brought Chango to her. As we drove away, Jesús and Flor told me that they found the place peaceful and beautiful. Jesús filmed out the window, much amused by a boy riding his horse straight down the steep embankment and into the canal.

We spent the rest of the day on the beach near Guaymas. It was the first time Jesús had been to the sea, and he watched with amazement as I swam out to a school of dolphins. "Watch out, Lorenzo!" he shouted. "Aren't those sharks?" We crowded together on a rock jutting out into the sea and watched a perfect scarlet bath of a sunset behind the returning shrimp boats.

The next morning we headed north again, speeding through the desert and dry hills toward the border. Somewhere in the middle of our journey, Ricardo, remembering our friend Boston's questions, asked Jesús if he had ever been in danger of death.

I looked in the rearview mirror to see Jesús' expression. He was serious and reflective, an arm draped gently over Flor, who was collapsed on his shoulder, sleeping.

"Yes," he said. "One time I came up on these two cholos, close to a hardware store. They looked at me and one of them said, 'Hey, *cholo cara de perro*—dog-faced cholo—where's the wallet you stole?' I told them that I didn't steal anything. Then they looked like they were going to hit me, so I pulled out a knife. And Chiguile, too—he was there with me. They started looking for a stick, but where would they find a stick there by the market in the center of town? So they fled."

"Another time," Jesús continued. "I was going to Tucson. I was on pills. I was coming from Nogales, Arizona, on the train, riding between the cars. Well, when those pills 'explode' on you, they knock you out. That's what happened to me, and I fell, but I gripped the bar and held it. My belly was scraped between the two cars, but if I had let go, I would have been cut in half like Ardilla. Three or maybe four of my friends have died like that or in the tunnel. A *pollero* with a pistol threatened me once, but afterward he calmed down. And the Beta, they used to shoot at us a lot."

I looked again at Jesús and Flor there in the back seat, star-crossed lovers on their way back from a romantic weekend on the seashore. "How did you meet Flor?" I asked him.

He gazed over for a moment at her gently sleeping form. "We met at Mi Nueva Casa. At first I only looked, but little by little we spoke. Then she ran away from home for a week. First, she was at Karin's home [another volatile beauty with whom the other girls later fell out], and then she went to Negrita's house. I saw her there. She told me that she needed a favor—that she needed diapers—so the next day I got six hundred pesos in the tunnel and bought clothes and diapers and all, and I went to Negrita's house. Negrita asked for some of the diapers for her sister. She and her husband were in jail, and Negrita was taking care of two kids. Anyway, the two of them were talking—Negrita y Flor—and Flor asked Negra who kisses better of the boys; the girls roll over several guys before picking one. And La

Negrita said that I kiss better. So then the day after I came there again and brought the diapers to Flor. She made the first move; she kissed me, and then I hugged her, and with that first kiss we started to go together."

How romantic, I thought. But Ricardo was still thinking of Boston's other questions. A few minutes later he asked Jesús, "If you were king of the world, would you want there to be cholos?"

It was Flor who answered; she had awakened in the meantime and was staring dreamily out the window again. "Who knows," she said. "Money changes people. People say they would help each other if they had money. But the rich don't give to the poor; they make themselves chiefs!"

"I would give to those I knew who needed it—who were very low," Jesús said.

"Jesús told us how you two got together," Ricardo said to Flor.

She looked over at him and laughed quietly, then told us her version. "We all went—Toñito, Ana, Jesús, and I—to the fair. That was the first time I went out with him, but I couldn't stand him. Later, I ran away from home. I went to Karin, but she kicked me out. Then I went to Negrita's house, and we were talking about who kissed the best, and Negrita said that Jesús was good, 'but he makes me sick.' One day I asked him to buy diapers for me, and he said yes, and when he came that evening, he just lay down on sofa outside. I sat beside him, and he put his hand on my leg, and then we kissed."

"Do you have any plans together?" Ricardo asked.

"I don't know. We are going to study and work. We used to work—at a coil factory. We worked from seven till five, so we had to wake up at three or four in the morning and walk from Los Virreyes. It was too difficult. A lot of guys were hanging out all night making noise, so we couldn't sleep enough. We missed two days that way, and they fired us. We were in training. We did a thousand pieces a month and fixed defective ones. We would correct them from other workers, but we were always too sleepy, and the work was too boring."

"Once I fell asleep and hit my head on the machine," Jesús added, laughing.

"We got food there," Flor continued, "but we had to pay for lunch. Breakfast was free."

Several weeks later, I was chatting with Flor in the little park by the bronze statue—the Dummy—when a darkly bronzed boy I did not recognize approached us.

"Lorenzo," he said, "don't you know me? I spoke with you in Barrio Yaqui, in Obregón with Chango." He had been the one asking me the price of clothing on the border.

"Yeah," he continued, "I came up here. . . . Have you heard about what happened to Chango's brother? He was killed, shot over drugs."

For a terrible moment, I thought that he had said that Chango had been killed, that I drove him—literally—to his death. I confess that I was relieved when I realized that it was not Chango who was dead, but his crazier older brother—someone I had not met and did not know.

It was not, however, the answer that I was hoping for to the question, "*¿De dónde eres?*"

SEVEN

LUGARES IMPORTANTES / IMPORTANT PLACES

After our return from Guaymas and Obregón, Flor began to show interest in the video camera and in the idea of recording herself and her friends. When I offered her a job helping me, she accepted happily. "I can interview everyone," she announced. No doubt she was thinking of Boston's questions from the year before, and, of course, like the others, she had seen enough TV to have a notion of the act—of the reporter shoving a microphone into some unfortunate's face and demanding answers to every sort of personal question.

In fact, her style was even more "professional" in that sense than Boston's. Once armed with the camera, Flor would begin a series of rapid-fire questions that, though never as probing as Boston's, would elicit biographical detail in a more effective way.

As in the time, only days after our return, when we decided on a break from the cruel noise and filth of Nogales. We were trying to find peace in the tiny municipal park right behind the Stupid Dummy when Guanatos said, "Do you know the arroyo beyond Solidaridad on the road to Cananea? It's not far from the city, but it is cool and beautiful."

That sounded good to me, so I looked around to see whom I might be able to fit in the car. There was, of course, Flor, Jesús, and Guanatos, but there was also Rebecca, who was slumped lethargically on the park bench next to Guanatos. Something was going on between them. She had arrived at Mi Nueva Casa only a few days before, from Culiacán—a notorious drug haven on the northern edge of the state of Sinaloa. Rebecca was a tall sixteen year old, with delicate features and hair piled on her nodding head. Still wearing the short bright blue summer dress in which she had arrived, she looked as if she had attended a teen party several days earlier and had neither washed nor slept since. In fact, she had spent the nights on the street and had, I assumed, sought out Guanatos as a protector. Not a bad move, I could not help thinking, given the choices. For the last couple of days, she had been sitting tentatively by his side, and Guanatos, for his part, had occasionally grazed her arm with his hand, but nothing more, at least in public.

Flor had at least once called Guanatos Rosa's boyfriend, though, and just when I was wondering what might happen on that front, Rosa herself arrived in the park, her two youngest children trailing behind her.

Jesús greeted his mother and told her that we were off to the arroyo, and she looked interested in going along, but Guanatos, who had shown little one way or the other up to this point, scowled and jumped into the car next to Rebecca and Jesús, who were already in the back seat, and slammed the door on the approaching Rosa. Flor climbed into the front seat next to me. Rosa was furious. Guanatos, whom I had seen only either sleepy or happy, barked angrily through the open window while I and everyone else stared straight ahead. Finally, Rosa strode away, and we pulled out into traffic.

I could not imagine what it meant to Jesús to see his mother in such dramas, but he gave no indication one way or the other. He and Guanatos asked for their favorite radio station, and both quickly settled into the music, singing along with Miguel y Miguel. Flor was interested in the video camera, which she fished out of its case. In a matter of seconds, she had mastered the controls and, wiggling around, pointed it over the seat at her boyfriend Jesús.

"Jesús," she said emphatically. "Do you know the countryside?"

To my surprise, he answered yes, that he lived for a while on *un rancho,* which led to a series of questions: "When? How old were you? How old are you now? [She must have been thinking of the home audience.] With whom did you live there? Who else? What did you do? How did you learn that?"

Jesús smiled shyly as he answered in short sentences, telling his inquisitor that at thirteen years of age—two years earlier—he had spent ten months with a grandfather and uncle following a life far removed from what he had known and further yet from his present pursuits. He had learned the ways of cows and the many tasks involved in their care. When I asked him if he had liked that life, if he missed it, he barely answered yes, still smiling. But then Flor asked him—still in professional interviewer mode—where the rest of his family was. He laughed and said, "In Nogales—*drogalito!*"

Six or seven wheel-wrenching miles later, we arrived at the arroyo—a dry riverbed, but with a smaller stream nearby that flowed with the summer rains. We all wandered over the cracked mud, chasing tiny toads as Flor continued to film and occasionally asked Jesús or Guanatos something about the local scene. Two large concrete pilings supporting an overpass were covered in graffiti. Guanatos explained that the artists were not members of Barrio Libre, but of another *pandilla* (gang) from Solidaridad. Flor took that statement as her cue for another interview. She settled herself next to Guanatos on the stream bank and asked him a series of staccato questions that led him to recount—however tersely—the story of his departure from the family home in Guadalajara and acceptance in the bosom of Barrio Libre.

"Do you have any family here in Nogales?" she asked. "No," he replied. "Only your friends, then?" she continued. "Yes," he answered, smiling for the first time in the recitation, "my friends—all those of Barrio Libre."

We lounged there for another peaceful hour, watching a huge buzzard float down on a nearby branch and listening to the music coming from a car radio a few yards away, where a large family was picnicking under a cottonwood grove.

On the drive back, Flor was back on duty with the video. She asked for songs and had no difficulty in eliciting ballads of lost love and daring drug adventures from both Jesús and Guanatos. Rebecca, whose head had lolled in the sun the whole way out, was awake now and enjoying the entertainment. She came totally alive, however, when Flor—having taped enough a cappella—flicked on the radio and turned up the volume for a series of popular love songs.

I'll never forget you, my love,
And now separated, my heart is dying, dying for love.

They all belted out the lyrics, Rebecca looking as if she were back at that imagined teen party and Guanatos hamming it up for the camera with hand flourishes and Latin lover eyes. Jesús sang along as well, but his attention drifted, and he contented himself with flashing a series of complicated gang signs for the camera as we bounced back through the edge of the city, passing through Solidaridad. A huge and friendly crowd was gathered as usual around the only source of water on that side of the *colonia:* a wide white-plastic pipe jutting from a dirt hillside, with two naked four year olds straddling it as if it were their pet pony.

Through the following days, Flor continued to accompany me around the city, often interviewing her friends in action. One afternoon she cornered the windshield washers under the Dummy.

Chito was there, along with a couple of his friends. In fact, I had been wondering and worrying about Chito. He seemed to have changed since the previous summer. Then, he was among the apparently brightest and certainly most buoyant of the kids. He spoke frequently and easily with me, telling me stories of his native Navojoa—to which he had invited me on several occasions—and of his hopes for a future as a bus driver. But this summer his mood was different. He had been arrested on both sides of the border and was convinced that one of the workers at the Casa had turned him in. He had avoided the Casa ever since, and when I saw him up at the casita or out on the streets, he was cordial but distant and a little wary.

But on this particular day he was so amused by Flor's interviewing technique that he leaned back against a parked car and spoke of the money they made and their techniques. He also introduced his two pals—Xavier and Armando. They were both neighbors from Navojoa who, like Chito, had been shuttling periodically the several hundred miles between Nogales and their *tierra* to the south. Their answers to Flor's questions revealed some of the complex differences among the kids: their circumstances varied widely, as did their adaptations to life here on the border. This Navojoa contingent formed a clear sub-group that cooperated closely and kept up a bond not only among themselves but also with relations back home. All three of them were in the habit of moving easily back and forth between "bases." "When it is hot up here," Chito said, smiling, "we go down to see what's going on there. But you can't make as much money in Navojoa, so we come back up to Nogales. And now we are here, but the tunnel is very difficult now. Nobody has been in it much for the last month or more, so we are washing windshields."

Flor had reopened my relationship with Chito, whom I went back to see the next day. He was there at his post, but was not himself. He was nearly swaying beneath the great bronze Dummy, paler than usual, although slightly flushed. I noticed for the first time how his long lashes curled away from his eyes. When I asked him how he was feeling, he told me that he wasn't well. "Just now I was sitting there on the curb for a moment, and I passed out and banged my head against the curb." I was worried, for it was very unusual for Chito—or any of the kids—to complain of illness. Though they often had stomach problems, probably the result of contaminated water, and were fairly frequent victims of relatively minor STDs, they seemed much healthier than one would expect. "I feel chills," he whispered, running his hand over goose flesh, "and pains here." He passed his hand in lithe gestures around his waist and back. I felt his forehead. "You have some fever—*calentura*." He agreed without moving and added, "I was hoping to get away, to take the bus down to Imuris. If it works out, Jesús will be there with his father."

"You can go later," I told him. "Now, you need to see a doctor." After a bit of coaxing, Chito agreed to go with me to Mi Nueva Casa. Our reception was not, however, encouraging. "It's a weekend," the ladies at the Casa said dismissively, rather unmoved by Chito's condition.

He had ceased to become a regular there, and Ramona and Loida assumed he was haunting the tunnels. I had told them that he had been bored by the fractured school lessons and ambitious to put in as many hours washing windshields as possible, but they had been skeptical.

Determined to get him some attention, I put Chito back in the car and took off for the Red Cross clinic. After an hour there I finally bugged an attendant enough to get Chito into an examination room, only to be told that a doctor might show up in a few more hours, but that we should not count on it. "If you want him to see a doctor," the sympathetic young man sporting a white coat told me, "I would advise you not to wait here, but to take him to the small public hospital, El Básico."

Never was a hospital better named. We walked in through the emergency entrance into a waiting room and found our places with half a dozen others—all women and children. The children squirmed and yelled, ignored for the most part by mothers who looked as if they had always been and would always be waiting where they sat, every one of them staring blankly at an empty, glass-windowed booth. Suddenly the doors banged open and a man of about thirty-five staggered noisily in and, leaning into the window, began talking fast and loud into the emptiness. "The police," he said, "have sent me to a place without doctors!" We all were in the same boat, but he did have a right to be agitated, I thought, when I saw that he was clutching a large ragged chunk of ice, taking it on and off an eye so swollen that it looked to be missing. Below, a sorry gash was still oozing blood. Disgusted, he left the room to try another glass door that led into the hospital corridor. "Let's follow him," I said to Chito.

So we found ourselves standing behind the man with the ice, who rattled at what appeared to be the main hospital door, except that it was bolted shut. Through it we saw a private security guard. I must have been getting accustomed to a certain level of weaponry by then because he did not look threatening to me with only a pistol and billy club. Behind him in the shadows, though, I could see another guard sitting quietly, nestling an assault rifle in his lap. The first guard opened the door, not for us, but for the iceman and about half a dozen metropolitan police whom I had not seen behind us. They pushed by and sauntered in slowly. Wisely or not, I grabbed Chito by the arm, and we followed everyone through the door to find ourselves in a kind of hall with a few cots. The assault victim was already stretched out on one of them, still clutching his dripping ice and leaning on one elbow. He began to tell his story to the police, several of whom were officiously taking notes.

I looked around in vain for anyone who might be medically trained. In the back corner, a receptionist was flirting with an orderly, while another guard passed like a ghost through the corridor beyond, a heavy rifle slung over his back as if he were guarding a field of marijuana or poppies deep in the sierra.

For no apparent reason, a nurse suddenly appeared before us, and when he heard Chito's complaints, thrust a thermometer under the boy's armpit. He walked away, but returned five minutes later with a round and jovial doctor—the first man I had seen there without a uniform, cell phone, or gun. He told the nurse that he would see Chito in a small consultation room, and we followed him in, only to find the last patient, an Indian woman, still within, lying on the cot in her hospital gown, a bag of saline solution hooked up above her. But she was unceremoniously hustled out, rolling her own iv set-up along with her as she trundled into the mayhem of the corridor. The doctor fell into his chair, looking at Chito, and then up at me.

"He is your son?" he asked. I was surprised at first, but realized that Chito was, if anything, lighter skinned than I was. I also realized that this fact was probably why we had been seen. But before I could answer, Chito told him that I was not his father, but rather a volunteer at Mi Nueva Casa. Thus, he identified himself as a street kid, and the doctor adjusted his manner accordingly. He asked the usual routine questions, took a few vital signs, and checked not only Chito's throat, but also his arms for signs of extracurricular drugs.

"I don't do that," Chito said calmly, "only marijuana, *la mota*, and paint, *las pinturas*." The doctor did not even bother to disapprove. He wrote out prescriptions for three drugs, and we found our way out and over to the pharmacy right across the street from the Stupid Dummy. A moment later, I stood out on the street with Chito, calculating the

Xavier

"damages:" ten dollars for the clinic visit and forty dollars for the medicine—a good week's wages in a *maquiladora*. Just then, Chito's pal and Navojoa countryman, Xavier, came along. He was clearly annoyed and a little scared.

"That fucker Marco," he said, looking down the street in the direction of a dangerous-looking man—in his late twenties with a mustache, earring, and bandana—who lounged with another thug on a stone balcony over a curio shop. "He sells heroin and is often in the tunnel," he tells me. "He is a mean bastard." He noticed Chito looking bad and clutching a little bag of medicines. "What happened to you, man?"

Chito told him that he was sick and had been hoping he could find a place to sleep. "How is the tunnel?" he asked him. "*¡Caliente!* Hot! Man, you can't go in there; it's crawling with Betas. I was there four or five days ago, with Toñito and some others—maybe there were five of us. Betas came in, and we got out fast."

The tunnel was out, so we took Chito into the little park behind the Dummy and settled him down on a bench to rest there.

Such were the limits of my success in trying to help the kids deal with the bureaucratic world around them. Nevertheless, encouraged by the promise Flor was showing in her interviews, I decided to make a more concerted effort to help her. I thought that the only long-range hope was more schooling, but that plan was not working very well for Flor or for most of her friends. For one thing, teachers were proving far too irregular at Mi Nueva Casa, and the kids were no surer in their attendance. They were not always up to the several-mile-long trek early in the morning, or the pressures of making money might take precedence. If Chito and his pals were out washing windshields all day to make enough money, would it be a good idea, I wondered, to get him into the schoolroom for the morning, leaving him only the afternoon to make a living in some faster and more dangerous manner? As for Flor, she was now frequently minding her own Davidcito in her father's house in Los Tapiros while her sister Myrna worked. She was better off there than the casita or the street, I thought, and if she had her own textbooks, perhaps she could make her way through at least the rest of her primary school training.

Ricardo the guitarist had had some experience with a few members of the local school bureaucracy, so we girded our loins and descended into the hallways and waiting rooms of that world with the aim of getting schoolbooks—especially for Flor and Jesús. After a series of long and pointless waits, we finally succeeded in tracking down the right official. "No Mexican child should be deprived of his education, no matter what the circumstances," said Señor Vargas to our surprise and delight, and sent for an assistant who piled texts and workbooks into our arms. We carried the lot to Flor's father's home in Los Tapiros and laid them in triumph on the table there.

Maybe we can help at least Flor, I thought, as she poured through the books with genuine excitement. I certainly had no doubt that she was smart enough to master the lessons, and during the next couple of weeks I frequently stopped in to visit her and find that she had in fact advanced in her studies. "Listen, Lorenzo," she would say, and she would recite or read or divide.

Flor remained interested in the video as well and suggested that we do some more filming in Nogales. I asked her and Guanatos to put their heads together and decide where we should go. In no time they came to me with a plan: "We'll go to important places—*lugares importantes.*"

So the next day Maeve got into the car along with us, and following Flor's directions we headed up the main *avenida* and then started climbing a steep hill, not into one of the poor colonias this time, but rather through the richest neighborhood in Nogales—Colonia Kennedy. The streets had names such as Athens, Sparta, and Thermopolae—given to them by the wealthy Greek merchants who had developed that part of town. I don't know how many of them lived there still, but they had been joined by another class of entrepreneurs who had made their money more quickly and with greater risk. The long houses of those drug lords squatted behind barbed wire–topped fences, crowned with radar dishes and endlessly circled by bands of loping black hounds.

"Pull over here," Flor said, and I did—along an actual, rare curb in what appeared to be a calmer section of a nearly American-looking upper-middle-class neighborhood with sprawling homes in various

designs. We followed Flor through an empty lot. She was clearly delighted to be leading the expedition.

"We would enter this way," she said, leading us over a mound of
loose sand and down a small hill. I could hardly believe my eyes.
There in the middle of posh Colonia Kennedy was a colossal ruin of a
house—a several-thousand-square-foot fantasy of cubes and domes
spreading over a hardened sandlot, perched on the cliff edge with a
beautiful view over the lots and houses of wealthy neighbors. A *nar-
cotraficante* Alhambra, but either unfinished or partly destroyed—it
was so difficult to tell the difference here. Outside were mostly bare
block walls. Inside, wherever the plaster wasn't removed, were intri-
cate overlays of graffiti—*placasos,* the names or signatures of the
kids. There were familiar names such as Pecas or Mr. Güero among the
many sprayed in gaudy blocks across the wall of what would have
been a central great room. The entire span of the opposite wall was
taken up by a name—or an expression of hope—in white paint: *Es-
peranza.* Beneath it was somebody's bedroom—a few layers of cardboard and old blankets, a hairbrush, and some magazines. Guanatos
picked up a broken straw hat with ribbons and placed it majestically
on Flor's head.

Flor gave us a house tour worthy of Century 21.

"We slept here and here," she said as we made our way out the
back to a stone porch overlooking a spread of mansions separated
by deeply cut washes. "I didn't yet have Davidcito. We would make
a fire and cook some things and amuse ourselves. How? We would
tell stories." In recounting those days—six or so blissful months it
seemed—Flor was dreamily nostalgic. "It was great here," she continued. Guanatos looked like he was ready to buy a condo. Then
Maeve set up her camera, and he and Flor posed together and sepa-
rately under graffiti, in doorways or on a ledge, always smiling and
arranging their fingers in the shapes of the letters B or L for Barrio
Libre.

I stood on the porch surveying the scene and wondering how
the presence of a gang of doped up street kids had been tolerated.
I asked Flor about the neighbors.

"The man next door would bring us water; this house belonged to a relation of his," she explained. I was imagining that there must have been a drug connection involved when suddenly Flor's narrative took a different tack.

"His nephew attacked me one time. He wanted me, and he would come over here and try to find me without the others. I got away from him many times. One time I couldn't get away."

She related that scarring episode flatly and then turned immediately back to happier memories of the free life of Barrio Libre in this unlikely setting. As we left, she looked back fondly, as if on a happy youth. "I did not know this place," Guanatos remarked with enthusiasm, "but I may come back with some friends!"

It was Guanatos's turn, and he directed us to the southern edge of the city. "In here," he told me, indicating the parking lot of a huge supermarket. In fact, I had been there several times. When I was roaming the city with some of the kids, we would sometimes go into that market and put together a picnic of hot tortillas, a cooked chicken, and some beans. But Guanatos led us across the road to a dirt hill sparsely covered with grass and stunted trees. Cars and trucks whizzed or rattled by on the road below as we made our way up a dirt path.

I heard a noise to my right and turned to see a man under a tree about ten feet away, asleep in a tattered plaid blanket. Then I saw that there were others, maybe half a dozen scattered over the hillside. Guanatos, noting our astonishment, said, "Yes, they sleep here, and so did I when I first came to Nogales four years ago. I was thirteen. I and two friends. We slept up here."

He led us further up the hill to a grassy glade sheltered by two fairly large trees. From that height we could see across the highway to the train station, no doubt Guanatos's port of entry to the fabled world of the border.

"Yes," Guanatos said, again guessing my thoughts. "We came in at the station, and the very first place I stayed was there—in a train car. But a *cholo* told us we could come up here. We stayed here three months, but then it got too cold."

While we were talking, Flor was, as usual, foraging. "Look," she said to Maeve, *"bellotas."* She pulled a handful of tiny gray nuts from the tree under which we were standing, and popped one in her mouth. One expert crunch and she spit out the shell and munched contentedly on what remained. "I love them," she announced simply.

Meanwhile, Guanatos had picked up a couple of spray paint cans from the grass nearby and, giving them a languid shake so that beads clanked against the empty chamber, looked up at us and smiled. "Still cholos coming here," he said.

"Where did you go next?" I asked.

"Let's go there. I'll take you."

So it was back to the car and then off again through the streets of Nogales, north again toward the center of town, where narrower, sometimes cobbled streets were lined with adobe and concrete homes and shops. Guanatos brought us to a house on a corner, from the outside a pretty pink adobe box with wrought iron work on the windows and door.

"*Abandonado,*" Guanatos said and nudged the door open with a shove of the shoulder. We followed him, Flor filming our entry and movement through four little rooms, every one of them empty, every wall covered with the placasos of compatriots and the initials B and L: Barrio Libre.

"How long did you live here?" Flor asked, back in *reportera* mode.

"We were here maybe six months," Guanatos answered, leaning into one of the doorjambs and looking about with a satisfied smile. "It was great. Humberto, Gilberto, and I were all here, and we had everything in the place. Everything you'd need." He walked over to one of the walls as he spoke and traced his finger over the graffiti names, pronouncing each one as if he were reciting a beautiful, evocative poem.

"We were great," he continued, "but then the police came, and they forced us out. Threw us into the street and boarded the place up. That is their way here, you know. They had no reason for doing it. They had taken the house from some drug dealer, so no one lived in it. And we didn't hurt anything—we made it better!"

A matter of perception, I thought, looking at the graffiti, but I also knew that there were many such houses, confiscated, empty, collapsing, all over a city with a critical shortage of housing.

HUMBERTO

"They threw us out," Guanatos repeated, "and they boarded up the place. 'If you come back in, we'll shoot you!'" he said, completing his rendition of police manners with a simulated pistol thrust into the air.

"And then," Flor asked, filming still, "where did you go after that?"

"Not far, just down the street."

We went on foot this time, a few picturesque blocks through a neighborhood poor but still clinging to a few scraps of old Mexico charm. We rounded a corner and found ourselves standing before a large structure: La Plaza de Toros—the bullfight arena. Above the entranceway, gay murals of fight scenes blistered in the sun. Maeve and I had attended a *corrida* (bullfight) there a few years earlier; I smiled to remember the señoritas with their great-brimmed hats and blood-red roses. But there were no more fights there—or at least not ritual contests between man and beast. Like the coliseums after the fall of the Roman Empire, this arena—abandoned by the toreadors, matadors, and fans—had been colonized by the poor. The rooms and corridors within the gates had been appropriated, boarded, or cordoned off into dozens of chambers and dens, within which family life was being noisily lived.

"Stupid! Stupid! Stupid!" It was the voice of a young girl whose face looked out at us through a slatted makeshift window cut through the arena wall. I looked in to see her naked form skip away laughing into the shadows.

"Over here," Guanatos said, leading us around the back of the arena to a trash heap replete with dozens of spray paint cans. He swept up four of them and with Flor's help gave us the principals of brand and color selection. "See, this is *dorado*—gold—that's the best. This kind is good. You get it at Wal-Mart on the other side. This other one you get around here, but it's not that good. This other one is expensive. It is easy to get any of them though." They were smiling as they told us all this, perhaps proud of their expertise.

But then Flor said, "It is very bad for you. It makes you crazy, and then you can't think straight. You can't remember things"—not the first time I had heard one or another of the kids say something similar.

I was never sure whether they were simply saying what they thought I would want to hear, but I suspect that they did think of the paint as destructive and bad, and that, at the same time, they liked and needed it. How many people, after all, are similarly conflicted about drugs, alcohol, cigarettes, or their lovers?

But the tour was continuing, and we followed Guanatos up the steep, trash-strewn slope along the side of the arena. Maeve and Flor waited outside, squatting in the shade, while I followed Guanatos on hands and knees through a low, narrow passageway in the wall. Inside, we were in total blackness—a dank and pungent cavity. I crouched frozen in complete disorientation, unsure of whether I was in danger of bashing my head on some possible ceiling or of tumbling into some yet darker, yet filthier pit below. When my eyes adjusted to the weak light, I saw that both possibilities had been real. We were sitting in a concrete chamber perhaps four feet high and six feet square; just beyond, the floor broke off to reveal a larger chamber be- low us—a good eight-foot drop to the next floor. I could also make out a sheet of cardboard that someone had dragged into the chamber in which we sat.

Guanatos looked around him. "We stayed here for a little while— some stayed longer—but I didn't. It was bad. Very bad. Dirty and many violent people around."

His comment awakened me to the risk we were all taking in crawl- ing around the place, and I scrambled out into the sunlight. But Maeve and Flor were happily waiting where we had left them—two beautiful woman chatting away about hair color as if they weren't sitting in the middle of one of the filthiest places on God's Earth.

There was, of course, only one place to go from there, and that is where Guanatos and Flor next led us. The entrance to the tunnel—the same one I had visited a year before with Boston—was where Avenida Tecnológico branched off from the main artery, only a few hundred yards from the old arena, the very middle of the city. We hopped over the wall and scrambled down into the dry arroyo, following Gua- natos—who by now acted the accomplished tour guide—into the tunnel. He pointed out the graffiti at the entrance, as had Boston and the others the year before, and, again like them, beamed with heartfelt pride.

Flor was happier than she had been all day. She nearly bounced up with excitement and offered to take us in deeper. We followed her and Guanatos, but slowly, letting our eyes adjust to the diminishing light. My other senses were not adjusting, however. The smell of human waste and rain-soaked trash was overwhelming, but I was distracted by fear. Maeve hung back a few yards taking photos while I edged out on the concrete shelf with Flor and Guanatos. I could hear and then see the stream of water flowing beneath us. The faint light disappeared to the north.

"Are there many girls in Barrio Libre?" I asked Flor.

"There are maybe ten," she replied, "and about thirty men, more or less."

"Yes," Guanatos added, "there used to be more, and more from Tucson's Barrio Libre, but not now. The *polleros*—they just take the people across, but we mug them, take their money. If they resist, we throw ourselves on them. Other gangs attack them as well—those from La Reforma, Buenos Aires."

He paused and then continued, warming to his memories of good times in the tunnel. "I used to take people across, too, for six or seven hundred. One time I met this guy with a thousand dollars. 'How much would you charge to cross me?' he asked. I made a deal to take him and his group across, so I said to the guy to give me all the money he was carrying because when you go through, someone will try to rob you. So they gave me all their valuables to hold. When we reached the other side, I returned the valuables, and I was about to give him the money when the *migra* showed up. They got him, and he lied, saying he was born in Los Angeles, so I kept the money! I bought clothing and shoes for my little sisters.

"Another time, Jesús and I were here in the tunnel together, with another guy who had cancer. Jesús had a watch, and the guy who had cancer took it from him, and he hit Jesús. He looked like he knew how to fight. I jumped in, but then the guy started screaming, 'Don't hit me. I have cancer!' He used to hang out with another guy from Guadalajara. He died." He paused only for a moment before continuing, "Many are gone now. Some are dead, many arrested, and a few have gone back to their own *terreno* [plot of land]. We had many good times here, but now it is very hot—it isn't cool."

When we emerged again into the shocking daylight and noise of central Nogales, Guanatos turned around and took another long look at the tunnel entrance.

"You see," he said, "the other kids from the colonias—those of Solidaridad or Los Tapiros or Buenos Aires—they have their places, their colonias, their pandillas that defend them. We have no place. We have nobody. We have nothing. *Nada de nada.* Absolutely nothing. For us, there is here—the tunnel. And we are different from them, too, because they boss each other around. The older ones order the younger ones and so on. We are all equal. No one of us is chief. No one tells the others what to do or where to go. That is the way we are."

EIGHT

"Don't they want to change? Don't they want a family, a home?"

Maeve and I had heard that question often enough from the people involved with Mi Nueva Casa. They were frustrated by the inconsistent, unpredictable behavior of the kids. "Why," they would complain, "do they show up for classes all enthusiasm, but then miss several days? They even disappear for a month or two—just when they seemed to be making progress."

Of course, the people running the Casa saw only a fraction of the kids' worlds. Not that we knew everything about the kids, far from it, but we had seen them in many more places and in many more situations, and had some inkling of the complexity of their lives. For them, the Casa was one element in a delicate adjustment to a world formed and manipulated by forces well beyond their control, if not beyond their ken. The brutal edge of those forces was typically manifest in the guise of men with guns: representatives of the U.S. and Mexican states or the criminal forces of drug and immigrant runners. All were there to protect the interests of free trade—a movement of electronic parts, grapes, drugs, or labor from Mexico into the United States. That movement was answered by a flow of money going the opposite direction in the forms of "legitimate" profits from *maquila-doras,* "illegitimate" profits from contraband, and emigrant remittances. This "exchange" was based in disparities and inequalities that were not about to disappear. Moreover, this world of powerful actors was, to make matters worse, unpredictable. Drug cartels and their local associates were subject to reorganization and realignment, and agents of the Mexican state might seem almost as volatile. U.S. enforcement of antidrug or immigrant control laws was also somewhat quixotic, subject to sudden bursts of activity in the form of legislation, movements of manpower, increases in technology. Among the representatives of this shifting if powerful world, the tunnel kids found enemies and untrustworthy friends, and they attempted to put together lives, families, and "clans" in the face of all that. The result was a powerfully imagined but loosely structured band, without the formal rituals or hierarchy typical of many street gangs.

And without a well-controlled territory. I kept thinking about Flor and Guanatos and their tour of *lugares importantes.* We had been shown more than a series of awful places in which they had stayed; we had been taken through their personal histories. Their experience of each place and of the people in it had been shaped by where and with whom they had been prior to that particular point in time. So, too, I realized, was their view of the present, of Mi Nueva Casa, of Maeve and of me. Their worlds could be totally encompassing, emotionally embraced, and passionately lived, but they were contingent, fragile arrangements of person and place, requiring performance and always subject to forces well beyond their control.

For the kids, Barrio Libre may have offered a constant cultural and personal identity over the last several years. It defined a somewhat bounded territory that went from South Tucson, across and under the border, through the city of Nogales, and on to the personal home bases scattered through Mexico. That territory was peopled—though very sparsely—by those they could recognize as their own. Their very movement through this world was part of their identity—part of their sense, however illusory, of "freedom"—but that physical and social world was very limited. Hostile forces, always capable of ousting them from one toehold or another, of course shared the territory.

Even the tunnel, which had been the most constant "place"—a home and anchor—was more and more too "hot" for them. With their graffiti, *los placasos,* the kids claimed places and spaces, attesting their own real presence there and helping to narrate a collective history in the confiscated, crumbling, derelict, and dangerous bits of Nogales that were left to them. As they swaggered proudly through this world or crouched in fear in its hidden corners, they reassured themselves with hand signs, knowing nods and signals, *cholo* clothes, posture, and movement. A necessary performance.

Even if well and convincingly performed, however, Barrio Libre could offer only so much. The actual struggle for survival was acted out in smaller groups, for the reciprocal exchange of aid, material goods, and love did not flow easily through that greater group. Scarcity, unpredictability, and the effects of drugs limited trust. Barrio Libre did not have meetings, organize activities, or hold rituals. It was rather an umbrella identity and category within which kids formed more real and much smaller associations: couples, such as Jesús and Flor or Fanta and Romel, or even little families with as many as eight or ten members. Such groups hung out and worked the tunnel or the Stupid Dummy windshield-washing "franchise" together. The clique of three pals from Navojoa was another such arrangement. The strength of such groups, however, depended at least in part on creating something like a home together. That much had been clear in the Flor and Guanatos tour. Each place they took us defined a group that hung together in that place and often for only as long as they could be there. The layers of graffiti on the walls were like archaeological strata, testifying to the passing of one "clan" and the arrival of another.

Knowing all this, of course, did not do much to help us solve the problems of any one person, such as Flor. She, like any of us, was a creature of contradictions—fully integrated into and very much needing this Barrio Libre world, yet also, at least at times, quite aware of its limitations and perhaps looking for a path that led out of it. But neither Mi Nueva Casa nor we had offered her more than scraps—certainly not enough to replace her own world, however patched together it might be.

La Flor

Flor had been keeping up with the schoolbooks and the video camera for a couple of weeks, though. One weekend late in that second summer, thinking perhaps of our trip to Guaymas and Obregón, she asked if we could go to Puerto Peñasco, a seaside town several hours to the southwest.

"I was born there," she told us, "but I can't remember it. We moved to Caborca when I was two and soon afterward to Nogales. My aunt still lives there, and I have an address, a phone number. We could find her."

There were many reasons to go. Thinking again of Flor's fractured family and history, I wondered whether this request could be her effort to deepen as well as strengthen a familial past and hence her sense of who she was. Instead of visiting an abandoned house in which she had lived with the gang for a few months, we were going to find the place of her birth, the terrain of a forgotten childhood, and if not rediscover her absent mother, then at least the mother's sister.

"Yes," I told her, "we'll go and see what we can find. Do you want to bring Jesús?"

She did, of course. But in the way of things in that world, Jesús was not there when we were preparing to leave on Saturday morning. Guanatos, she said, was available for the trip, though. So off we went to El Tío's Llantera, where we found Guanatos dressed, groomed, and packed for the excursion. He had been staying there for some time, I knew—a hopeful sign. Like Chito's bus driver friend in Navojoa, El Tío was a combination boss/father figure who had given Guanatos a job helping to repair tires and was also building a tiny cinder block bedroom for him in the corner of the lot. "In the meantime," Guanatos had told us, "I am sleeping in the truck."

But just when we were about to leave, Flor asked Guanatos, "Did you hear that they burnt down Rosa's *casita?*"

My hand froze on the keys. I couldn't believe my ears, not least because she reported this event with complete calm. I eyed the two of them in the rearview mirror.

Guanatos nodded slowly. "I am not surprised. There were problems—fights from before with others in the *colonia*. One of the cholos from there did it."

"Yes," Flor agreed. "They think it was someone from there. Before that, they had broken the doors and windows, and then this happened. They saw that the casita was left alone, and they burned it."

But then Guanatos said, "They didn't like us because we were crazy. The small drug dealers did it."

"Uh huh," said Flor. Looking moodily out the car window, she added, "*Pobrecito*. Poor Jesús. Yesterday we were like sweethearts, and yesterday we ended."

Guanatos was looking at Flor with what appeared to be sympathy. "Rosa didn't want you and Jesús in the house," he said, "and now you see what happened."

"I am better in my own house," Flor replied.

"Me too," Guanatos added, "that's why I came here with El Tío."

"But you were there at the casita the other day," Flor said, not quite accusing.

"And you were there every day!" Guanatos reminded her with a wry smile.

"That was before. I haven't been there for a month."

I had been sitting silent through the conversation, not yet starting the car, which was still parked outside the llantera. I turned around to look at Flor and Guanatos, and asked, "Where will they all sleep now—Rosa and the children?"

"Farther up in Virreyes," Guanatos replied matter-of-factly, "or else in Solidaridad. They will build another casita maybe."

Flor was getting restless; now she wanted to leave. She took out a wrinkled scrap of paper and said, "I have brought the telephone number of my mother, my aunt, and my half-sister Reina de Guadalupe, and my brother, Arón. He is ten years old."

"What if they kick us out?" Guanatos asked.

"No, they love me so much," she replied.

I started the car, wondering about all the possible consequences of this latest development in all their lives. I frankly did not know whether to be sad or glad. Of course, I was sorry for Jesús' younger brothers and sister, and even for Rosa, as well as about the destruction of yet another fleeting attempt—however problematic—to make a home. But perhaps both Flor and Guanatos were liberated from a place—and a person—holding them back from better things. If Guanatos was living and working at the llantera and Flor was now proud of her "home" and anxious to find the farther flung parts of her family, then maybe something good would come of all this change.

But before we could pull away, Rosa arrived, striding determinedly around the corner and up to our car. She had the two little ones in tow, and Alonzo ambled at his own pace behind. Guanatos got out of the car to talk to her, and in a moment he was back, saying that he would stay to help Rosa. He seemed proud of the sacrifice he was about to make in staying and of his role as the "man" who was needed to sort things out.

"Are you sure?" Maeve asked him. We were worried not only about his relationship with Rosa, but that he might seek revenge in the colonia. But Guanatos was calmly adamant, and Flor was getting anxious that the trip would be abandoned. I was wondering whether it wouldn't be good to take another of the kids along for the ride, however, so we circled back to Mi Nueva Casa and sent Flor in to find a traveling companion. She emerged with Diana, a girl she barely knew. Diana had just arrived in Nogales—a dark hermetic waif from San Blas, near Los Mochis in the state of Sinaloa. The two girls got into the car, Flor aglow with anticipation to visit her *tierra natal,* Diana somewhere between scared and happy, but mostly confused. One moment she was on the mean streets of Nogales and the next off with us on a trip to the seashore.

The journey south was uneventful enough. As we passed a large hotel on the southern edge of the city, Diana told us that she had stayed there. We looked at her with surprise and then realized that she had meant that a "john" had taken her there. She was fifteen now, she told us, and although she spoke of a *pollero* boyfriend, she had been living on the streets for the last few days and looked it. She was very dark from the sun, and her jeans were held together with a safety pin.

When we turned west at Magdalena, the more frequent signs for Caborca prompted more excited memories and speculation from Flor.

"I don't know Puerto Peñasco," she said, "because I was only two when we moved from there to Caborca. When I was five, they brought me to Nogales. I remember Caborca; it was so pretty. My father took me there. He and my mother never lived together, and she left me with him. His people were in Caborca—grandpa, grandma, and others. Then he brought me away to Nogales, and my sister went away to work. But I remember Caborca."

The straight desert road took us quickly to that old mission town. When we stopped for a snack, Flor decided that she wanted to try to find her old house. Three or four times she was sure we had found the right street—the name of which she could not remember—but each time she was wrong. Asking for directions on corners did not help, so we eventually gave up and rolled on toward the coast.

Puerto Peñasco, like many resort towns in Mexico or the Caribbean, consists of two parallel and quite different worlds. With the closest beaches to Tucson and Phoenix—from which it is only three to four open road hours and with no Mexican customs or immigration to clear—Rocky Point (as it is known in the United States) has many seaside resort hotels crammed with gringos and, to a lesser extent, with well-to-do Mexicans. There is even a village of rustic beach houses huddled in the dunes just north of the town that is peopled mainly by snowbirds from Wisconsin. But the town itself, beginning one block beyond the tourist strip, is a grid of wide dirt roads lined with the modest homes of the several thousand Mexicans who live and work there.

As the sun began to set in a blood red sky, we drove up and down those dusty roads searching for Flor's relations. The phone number she had was neither her mother's nor her aunt's, but the number of someone who knew them and had a phone. From that person Flor had received directions; half an hour of circling in the car had not yielded results, however.

"Here, here," Flor said as we passed a small house with a high fence and a derelict station wagon collapsed like an old burro before it. I was skeptical, but when we got out of the car, a crowd of people from across the street came out to meet us.

"You are looking for María and Laura?" a round little woman asked us, looking at Maeve and me with something like wonder. "They are gone. They left a few days ago and will be gone for a couple of weeks."

While Maeve and I stood ready to cry in frustration, Flor explained who she was.

"Then I am your aunt," the woman said. "My brother is your aunt's husband." That seemed to reassure Flor, and I was certainly ready to accept the discovery of any friendly relation as a victory.

"Where are they?" I asked Flor's newfound kin. "Flor's family?"

"Near Nogales," the lady answered, "they are at the *ejido* by the '21' selling *bellotas*. They go up there every summer to sell them after the harvest." That was the second time that day I could not believe my ears. That we had just missed Flor's family by a day or so was just bad luck, but that they were just outside Nogales—where they went every year—was more irony than I was ready for. "Ejido" usually refers to a small rural community with cooperatively owned and farmed land, and the "21" was the customs station at which we had been obliged to wait a few hours that very morning. Flor looked stupefied, and Diana seemed to be in a trance.

"Well," I suggested finally, "we might as well stay here for a couple of days and enjoy the sea. Flor, you can get to know your tierra natal. Then when we return to Nogales, we can stop at the ejido and find your family."

"The girls can stay here with us," Aunt Isabela offered and then turned to Flor. "You and your girlfriend can stay here. You are family." The offer seemed very sincere, and Isabela's young children—Flor's cousins—were clearly delighted at the prospect of these exotic and beautiful teenagers spending a couple of nights. They led us past more dead or dying cars and circling animals into a cool adobe cottage. We left the girls happily chatting over a stack of tortillas at a Formica table in an immaculate kitchen, the dark green walls decorated by religious pictures and a portrait of Walt Disney's Goofy.

We picked them up the next morning and went to the shore, where Flor and Diana played in the surf and roamed the beaches, no doubt discussing their adventures in the rural disco to which Flor's newfound cousins had directed them the night before. In the evening, we found a hilltop restaurant with a patio view over the twinkling lights of the town and the twilight purple sea. Diana and Flor had fixed themselves up for the occasion—their hair piled up on their heads and Diana's dark lips luminescent with moon-white frost lipstick. They took photos of one another, and Maeve captured the two of them positively glowing in the starlight on a flight of stone steps.

As we ate, Flor looked out over the scene with immense pride. "This is my tierra natal," she said, "but there is *poca tierra. ¡Mucha agua!*"

I told her that she was right; there was little land and much water, but then that made it her *"agua natal."* Flor laughed at that figure of speech and then in a more serious mood, but still beaming, she asked all of us whether Puerto Peñasco was more beautiful than Nogales. It was not difficult to agree that it was much prettier in every way, but Flor was not satisfied. "Is it nicer than Guaymas?" she asked, thinking of the only other seaside town she had seen. "Yes, it is," we affirmed. "But is it the most beautiful place you have ever been?" Looking from her radiant face to the starlit sea, it did seem, at least for that moment, to be so.

On Monday morning, we began the journey home, stopping in Caborca again for a roadside feast of barbecued chicken and a look at the seventeenth-century mission, where Maeve set up tripod and camera for an impromptu photography lesson. Suddenly, however, a dust storm descended like a hellish whirling shroud over the entire town and drove us choking and laughing into the car.

As we approached Nogales, Diana slept and Flor became moody. I asked her whether she was happy to have met her relations in Puerto Peñasco.

"Those are not my people. I don't know them," she replied, staring out the window as the endless desert rolled by.

But when we arrived at the ejido, everything changed again. From the highway, it looked like a deserted, overgrown, used car lot: rusting trucks, station wagons, and a few extra-long Chevies scattered about under spreading trees. We made our way past them to find one house sitting in the midst of what seemed a Gypsy encampment. There were several large, open-fronted tents, and a couple of dozen people were lying about, inside and out. Three women stood around a large, rusted oil drum oven, searing huge, paper-thin Sonoran wheat flour tortillas. They looked up at us with the amazement our presence deserved. When Flor explained who she was looking for, however, their creased faces broke into huge grins, and the eldest shouted over toward one of the pickup trucks. The truck was loaded with several great burlap sacks of *bellotas,* against which were leaning an older man and woman.

"That is my *tía,*" Flor said, just as the woman stepped up to us and caught her wayward niece in a fat-armed embrace. Tía Laura looked up and told us that it had been some years since she had seen this one. We explained that we had been to Puerto Peñasco looking for them.

"You found us here!" she said. "Her mother is not here, though. She is in Hermosillo, working." She then called over toward the tents, "Reina de Guadalupe, come! Your sister is here!"

A plump dimpled girl of about eleven came running to us and fiercely embraced her half-sister. Flor seemed very happy to see her as well, and within seconds her extravagantly named little sister was ushering her around the camp and introducing her to all and sundry. "This is my sister!" she announced again and again. Then seized by a sudden idea, she nearly dragged Flor out of the camp and out onto the shoulder of the highway. In the distance, a boy was walking our way with a sack over his shoulder.

Following Reina de Guadalupe, who was shouting "Arón, Arón," Flor ran toward the boy, who finally stopped and stood waiting.

"This is your sister!" the little girl instructed her younger brother in a voice that demanded the proper emotional reaction. He smiled somewhat shyly and shook Flor's hand. Then, still under Reina's direction, the three strolled arm-in-arm back to the camp.

Maeve and I busied ourselves talking with the aunt and uncle about their pursuits. Every year, so they told us, they would gather the bellotas from trees near Puerto Peñasco and then bring them here to sell by the plastic sack to the people waiting to clear customs at the "21." We smiled, remembering Flor's taste for those nuts. She had picked them from the trees wherever we happened upon them, and Maeve had bought her a bag of them at that very customs station a few days before on our way south.

Suddenly, Flor appeared by our side, saying that we could go.

Diana, who had said little and hardly interacted with anyone there, was already in the car. So it was off on the last brief leg of our journey.

Diana asked for the radio to be turned on, and in a moment the two girls were singing along with the usual desperate love song: *"Te quiero. Te quiero. Mi corazón está muriendo de amor por ti."*—"I love you. I love you. My heart is dying of love for you."

The sentiment reminded me of some of Boston's final questions—about boyfriends and girlfriends, love, and marriage. I asked Flor who would be the man of her dreams.

"I want a man who would treat me well and love me a lot," she replied with feeling.

"And would he be rich? Would he give you things?" Maeve asked.

"No," she answered emphatically, "nothing material because the material does not last—*se acaba pronto*—while true love lasts forever!"

"What about you, Diana?" Maeve asked. "Do you think about getting married?"

"Yes, to my boyfriend. He's in Nogales," she answered, "When I was in El Cotume [juvenile detention]—that's where I met Flor—he got me out. But I don't want to get married till I'm eighteen. I was pregnant, but I had a miscarriage two months ago. The *papá* was a guy from Sinaloa." Diana was saying more than she had in three days. She continued, "My sister just arrived here from Sinaloa. I left home because I was jealous of her."

But Flor was still thinking about love. She said, "Love is something *bonito* that two people have to share, and they must be respectful of each other." She paused and then continued, clearly referring to Jesús, "I love him still so much. I would try to make him feel good, by my side, and do everything to make him happy. And if I asked him advice, as a wife, as a friend, he would help me. And I would give him advice. And he would see that I would do nothing against his family, but was there to make him feel good. If we had a good relationship—normal—then I would make him feel good, and we would get ahead in life. And if he wants a son, with the help of God, there we would be together, the four of us: Davidcito, the new one, Jesús, and I. To be happy you need to love and respect one another. Alone, how can you be happy? How can you have enough courage to get ahead? How can you have the will to live?"

It was a stunning speech, delivered quietly, dreamily, to us and to herself. Her words were filled with pain and, perhaps, hope. I wondered whether rediscovering a family there had given her the will to forge her own.

"Now that you have seen your relations here," I said, "your sister and brother and aunt, you can easily visit them. The city bus goes to the ejido, so you can see your sister again soon!"

But she answered, "*No voy a visitar. Ya lo vi.* I am not going to visit. I have already seen her."

The next day we were back at Mi Nueva Casa. Flor was there, still delighted with her visit to her tierra natal—she made us tell everyone there how beautiful it was—and still unmoved by her reunion at the "21."

"Let's film more," she suggested, and once again we went out, heading for the Stupid Dummy to see who was there and to find out what had transpired during our absence. Chito's friend Xavier was there, and so was Jesús. If he and Flor had broken up, there was no sign of it now. They told us that Guanatos had gone with Rosa and her children to a shelter in Colonia Buenos Aires. We decided to visit them, but first to go by the site of the former casita.

All that remained was a charred square—scorched bits of board sprinkled with melted lumps of plastic, colorful shreds of clothing, bed springs, and, miraculously, one folding chair sitting upright where it had been before the fire.

"What do you think happened, Jesús?" I asked.

"I don't know . . . we will make another house in Solidaridad," he replied, but his face was not hopeful. He wandered about the site in his Tommy Hilfiger shirt and baggy pants, nudging wreckage with his foot, while Xavier found a seat on a nearby pile of stones and looked out over the hostile neighborhood. I joined him there, and Xavier surprised me by saying that drugs had brought all this on. "Drugs are the problem. They are my problem. But the worst is Jesús' brother, Alonzo. He is crazy with them. It will kill him." Just then, Jesús walked by as if in a dream, humming another song of lost love.

The summer was coming to a close. I felt that I had gotten more and deeper answers to Boston's questions, that I could see and understand much more of the kids' street life. On the other hand, we had also become much more thoroughly enmeshed in efforts to help them, and on that score the picture was not very encouraging.

The only one who seemed to have made a strong move away from Barrio Libre, drugs, and the tunnel was Fanta—or Verónica, as she was still calling herself. She was not only going to beauty school, but also working in the evenings at one of the maquiladoras while her mother watched the kids back in Solidaridad. She was still with Romel, though, sleeping in the car. We worried that he was no better than he had been and that she had taken on too much.

Vero was optimistic, however, and enthused for days about an upcoming "Open Day" at her school, where she would demonstrate her new skills. She was anxious that we all attend, so we did. It was a festive occasion, but Maeve and I were surprised to discover that although Vero was the student with the least financial and social advantages there, she was also the most normal in terms of intelligence. Every other kid was at least mildly mentally disabled. Nevertheless, she seemed unaffected by that fact and proudly performed all the hair treatments she had learned.

She was, however, I learned that same afternoon, still furious with Flor, who had never paid her the two hundred pesos she owed. My heart sank when I heard this news because I had in fact paid Flor that amount for her help with the video camera, and she had gratefully agreed to pay her debt, even acknowledging that it would be dangerous for her not to do so. The determined anger in Vero's eyes convinced me that she was telling the truth, so I thought I would have to confront Flor about the matter the next morning at her father's house in Los Tapiros, where we had arranged to meet to work on the next installment of our film.

"I haven't seen her. She told me she was sleeping at a girlfriend's, but she didn't come home. Not for days. She is a liar. Don't you know that?" Flor's father spoke with complete resignation, looking at me as though I were impossibly thick. I looked over at the stack of schoolbooks on the table and, nodding politely, left.

I headed for the Stupid Dummy, but when I reached the junction with Avenida Tecnológico, where the road passed over the arroyo and the entrance to the tunnel, I spotted Guanatos and Rosa, and her two little ones, sitting on the wall. I pulled over and joined them, just as everyone else arrived from around the corner—Jesús, Alonzo, Chito, Xavier, Rebecca, and Flor—all of them carrying plastic bags full of clothes. Flor came up to me with tears in her eyes and held my hand.

"I am sorry, Lorenzo. I am sorry. I have disappointed you, I know. I have disappointed you. Do you still like me? You don't like me now, right?"

I told her that I still liked her and that I would no matter what she did, but that I still wanted to help her.

"What about your medical problem?" I asked her. A doctor had found a cyst that needed urgent attention, but like many people who feel no pain, I think she had difficulty believing the diagnosis. At any rate, she had no intention of keeping the appointment we had made for her.

"I am going with them," she said.

"Where?" I asked.

"We will go to Guaymas—or maybe Tijuana," said Guanatos, who had drifted over to us. They were all smiling at the thought of the adventure. I stood, only stunned for a moment by this latest plan.

We all sat on the wall over the tunnel entrance, and looking down into it, I thought of one last thing I could ask them. "Could you make a map of the tunnels?" I asked.

"Of course," Guanatos said, so I took a few blank pages from a notebook and taped them together to make a long sheet. Guanatos took it from me and spread it on the sidewalk, grasping the pen I gave him and squinting back and forth between the world around us and the blank paper. He began to draw. As he did, Chito and Jesús leaned over his shoulders, adding names and correcting lines. All the others watched with fascination as the map took shape before our eyes. There was the border, here ran the dry tunnel, here the wet one. All the while, below us men went in and out of the actual tunnel to use it as a lavatory. Flor filmed the whole event, and the little kids scrambled around us, watching the boys do the map and craning for a look at the camera. Passers-by on the street looked at us with some amazement: "Who can that gringo be in the midst of that crowd of street kids and the toothless crone of thirty-five, and what was the dark chola filming?"

I looked up to see that the sky was blackening. As Flor filmed Alonzo sitting in a tree branch and flashing his Barrio Libre hand signs, we were all startled by the long bolts of gleaming, almost green lightning soon followed by a booming crash of thunder.

The rain came, and I offered to take them in the car to the bus station, about a mile and a half up the road. Miraculously, we fit everyone in, the little ones on top of the big ones, the trunk filled with their windshield-cleaning equipment and plastic or tote bags crammed with a few scraps for yet another voyage—another commute probably to Guaymas or possibly to Tijuana.

So all eleven of us went sailing up Avenida Obregón, past the police who didn't care. "Let me drive my car," said Alonzo, clutching a Coke can; it was a running joke between us. But this time he added, "When you return, I tell you, I will no longer be alive." Chito asked when I would come again to Nogales. "Can you ask Maeve to send me more pictures of myself?" Guanatos asked. "Just have her send them to El Tío Llantera."

They all got out at the bus station and stood in the rain, taking proper Mexican leave with *abrazos* (hugs) and *besos* (kisses). Rosa made for the bus. She looked even worse than usual, with her three remaining top teeth glinting below bloodshot eyes and dirt-streaked hair. She was an unlikely mother or lover, I thought, but something of both for them and better than nothing. The others picked up their belongings and trooped after her. Jesús turned toward me and said, "*Cuidado,* Lorenzo"—take care—and Flor gave me one last enigmatic and soulful look, and then, breaking into a broad smile, ran after Jesús and his mother.

ABOUT THE AUTHORS

MAEVE HICKEY is an artist and photographer. She has exhibited both sculpture and photography extensively in Europe and the United States, and is represented in collections on both continents. She is the coauthor, with Lawrence Taylor, of *The Road to Mexico* and *Ambos Nogales: Intimate Portraits of the U.S./Mexico Border.* Hickey lives and works in her studio overlooking the River Liffey in Dublin.

LAWRENCE TAYLOR is a writer and anthropologist. He is the author of *Dutchmen on the Bay, Occasions of Faith: An Anthropology of Irish Catholics,* and, with Maeve Hickey, *The Road to Mexico* and *Ambos Nogales: Intimate Portraits of the U.S./Mexico Border.* He is Professor and Head of the Department of Anthropology in the National University of Ireland, Maynooth, in County Kildare, Ireland.